RIGHTLY DIVIDING THE WORD OF TRUTH

II TIMOTHY 2:15 "STUDY TO SHEW THYSELF APPROVED UNTO GOD, A WORKMAN THAT NEEDED NOT TO BE ASHAMED, RIGHTLY DIVIDING THE WORD OF TRUTH."

GALATIANS

FOR US COMMON FOLKS©

Written by: Christopher E. Howe

This book is dedicated to all those that may read these books to help you to see God on a whole new level than ever before.

All scripture references are from the King James Version of the bible. The scripture references are bold, capitalized, or underlined for emphasis. If a word is italicized, it is to indicate how it is written in the KJV

Index

INTRODUCTION

Galatians was written to the Christians in the church that Paul had started on his first missionary Journey. It was the church at Galatia, an ancient city in what we know today as Turkey. This church was founded by Paul, he had trained and taught the people there what it was like to be Christian and to live for the Lord.

Though they did not have the completed Holy Bible that we do today, they did have scriptures and that was to be their guide. The bible clearly tells us that our faith comes from the word of God, these folks in this church needed to rely on their faith and keep searching the scriptures, they had to stay the course. It is so easy for Christians, even those like me who are dogmatic bible believing Christians to get out of fellowship with the Lord.

This church had done just that, they had gotten themselves out of fellowship with the Lord, and then sin started entering into this church. I just wrote a book called “unguarded gates, The Local church” it is about this very subject and how as we are told in the New testament that the gates of hell will never prevail against Jesus’ church and that we as Christians are to guard those gates. It is our responsibility to not allow sin into our private lives, into our family lives, and into our churches. Once sin is allowed to enter in, then as I have been saying lately, “anything goes”

This church had quickly fallen away from the teachings of Paul and the scriptures by allowing the false doctrines into this church. There were those with ulterior motives that came into this local church, they came in and listened for a bit, they slowly caused contention, sowed discord, and this contention and discord was not dealt with and removed from them, and the next thing you know the church has left the teaching of the scripture and their faith was now shaken.

This lack of faith had this church begin to doubt Christianity, the authority that Paul had, as he has to defend this authority in a few of the verses here. Paul sends them this letter maybe in anger, but for sure in a state of a broken and frustrated heart. I know from being a Pastor that in ministry one can suffer from a broken heart and that sometimes those wounds take a long time to heal, however we must keep on keeping on.

Paul with his broken and frustrated heart wrote this letter to this church, telling them they had left the gospel of Jesus Christ for a false doctrine and that they need to get back on the path to the Lord. Oh how this is so similar to the churches in the United States today, oh how we have many, many, churches that are so like this church in Galatia that they have followed after a different doctrine other than Jesus Christ and him crucified. We must remember my dear reader friend, that any bible, book, religion, denomination, that preaches or teaches anything other than Jesus Christ as the only way to heaven is a lying, two-faced, Satan worshiping, lake of fire bound false gospel and needs to be removed.

Enjoy the book and remember, as always, my books are just studies that I have done in these bible books and are NOT, I repeat, are NOT to replace you actually reading the bible for yourself, and doing your own study. These are just my study notes.

You are loved

Pastor Chris Howe

CHAPTER ONE

Galatians 1:1-24

Paul, an apostle, (not of men, neither by man, but by Jesus Christ, and God the Father, who raised him from the dead;) And all the brethren which are with me, unto the churches of Galatia: Grace be to you and peace from God the Father, and from our Lord Jesus Christ, Who gave himself for our sins, that he might deliver us from this present evil world, according to the will of God and our Father: To whom be glory for

ever and ever. Amen. I marvel that ye are so soon removed from him that called you into the grace of Christ unto another gospel: Which is not another; but there be some that trouble you, and would pervert the gospel of Christ. But though we, or an angel from heaven, preach any other gospel unto you than that which we have preached unto you, let him be accursed. As we said before, so say I now again, If any man preach any other gospel unto you than that ye have received, let him be accursed. For do I now persuade men, or God? or do I seek to please men? for if I yet pleased men, I should not be the servant of Christ. But I certify you, brethren, that the gospel which was preached of me is not after man. For I neither received it of man, neither was I taught it, but by the revelation of Jesus Christ. For ye have heard of my conversation in time past in the Jews' religion, how that beyond measure I persecuted the church of God, and wasted it: And profited in the Jews' religion above many my equals in mine own nation, being more exceedingly zealous of the traditions of my fathers. But when it pleased God, who separated me from my mother's womb, and called me by his grace, To reveal his Son in me, that I might preach him among the

heathen; immediately I conferred not with flesh and blood: Neither went I up to Jerusalem to them which were apostles before me; but I went into Arabia, and returned again unto Damascus. Then after three years I went up to Jerusalem to see Peter, and abode with him fifteen days. But other of the apostles saw I none, save James the Lord's brother. Now the things which I write unto you, behold, before God, I lie not. Afterwards I came into the regions of Syria and Cilicia; And was unknown by face unto the churches of Judaea which were in Christ: But they had heard only, That he which persecuted us in times past now preacheth the faith which once he destroyed. And they glorified God in me.

COMMENTARY

1:1 Paul, an apostle, (not of men, neither by man, but by Jesus Christ, and God the

Father, who raised him from the dead;) As we will see in this book of Galatians that Paul was upset with the church there because of how fast they had drifted from the scriptures and the things of God. So he is re-establishing his authority to them as an apostle, as a man that God had ordained, chosen, to do what the Lord had told him to do.

Notice here Paul clearly states that he is first of all an apostle, remember one of the requirements of being an apostle is that they must have physically seen Jesus after his resurrection, which Paul did on his Damascus road encounter. Second, we see that Paul clearly states that he is NOT an apostle by any man or anything that man could do to make him one. In today's world there are many people, especially in the charismatic religion that call themselves apostles, however according to the Holy Bible they are wrong as they have never seen Jesus in the flesh.

The last thing Paul is clearly stating here is that he was made, ordained, an apostle by Jesus Christ himself, and Paul goes on to show that Jesus Christ was raised from the dead by God himself which proves that Jesus has risen from the grave. This is the authority as to which Paul is speaking to the church here at Galatia.

1:2 And all the brethren which are with me, unto the churches of Galatia: Paul is letting the reader know that at the time this letter was written, it was written to the church at Galatia, for us today it is us that are saved. Paul says that he is writing this letter, and that he, along with other apostles and brethren are supporting his letter. Paul is basically letting this church know that he and others backing him are all in agreement with what is being written here.

1:3 Grace be to you and peace from God the Father, and from our Lord Jesus Christ, Paul is coming to them respectfully, with compassion, and in the love of the Lord. He wishes them well; he wants them to have the peace from the Lord that they and all believers can have by walking in the spirit and not in the things of the world.

Paul is telling them that he not only wants the peace for them from God but also from Jesus Christ who as we know from the book of Matthew is the founder of the church as the body of Christ, and the local church, and he uses the apostles to get the local churches planted in these areas.

1:4 Who gave himself for our sins, that he might deliver us from this present evil world, according to the will of God and our Father: The authority is not being placed on Paul here but on Jesus Christ which is who we should still be placing the authority on today. Oh, how man has so taken that authority and placed it on themselves which is part of the mess we are in in our churches today.

Jesus Christ died on hat cross to save us, the believers, from our sins, Jesus took that sin debt that we could not possibly pay, and he who had no sin paid that debt for us. Jesus did this because it was God the father that loved his people so much that he was willing to offer himself as God the Son Jesus Christ to go to that cross for us.

Just remember this my dear reader friend, Jesus did not have to go to the cross he chose to go to the cross for you and for me. What authority this gives for Paul as he is writing this letter.

1:5 To whom be glory for ever and ever. Amen. Paul let's all power, glory, and authority rest on Jesus Christ while at the same time in the previous verses he has established his own authority under the Lord's authority. Just as God has placed me at Bethel as the authority of that local assembly in the physical realm, Jesus is the head of that church in all realms especially the spiritual realm. God has always used willing, obedient, fully surrendered, people to do what he has for them to do, and he provides, backs, and supplies all that that willing servant does for him.

1:6 I marvel that ye are so soon removed from him that called you into the grace of Christ unto another gospel: Paul begins to express his frustration with this church as he is saying that he is absolutely amazed how fast they left the faith of the gospel, their faith in Jesus Christ for a false gospel. When people enter churches, if they are not watched, and the fruit is not from the Lord, the church and Pastor must pray for spiritual discernment and correct and if necessary, remove that false teaching as soon as possible from the church so the people do not follow after it.

There are many people in this world today that are followers, they will follow whoever is speaking to them at that time. Most of these people do not make their own decisions, they do not know what is right or wrong nor do they actually care, they have been taught that following the crowd is what needs to be done. Just remember this my dear reader friend the bible tells us that broad is the way to destruction and many there be that go therein. (Matthew 7:13)

This church here was not grounded enough in the bible, they were not strong in their faith, so they followed whatever came along. The bible is very clear that one's walk with God has to be an intentional walk, it is not just going to church that makes you grow in the Lord, it is not the Pastor pounding you every week about the faith in the Lord, it is you that must draw nigh to God so he can draw night to you, it is you that must seek him early so you can find him. Once you begin to do that you will find the Lord, your faith will endure, and you will remove any and all false prophets and teachings from your life.

1:7 Which is not another; but there be some that trouble you, and would pervert the gospel of Christ. Pervert simply defined is: *to cause to turn away from what is true.* This verse says that there were some in this church that caused the message of the gospel to be perverted, the message that these false teachers were teaching was turning the people in this church away from the gospel of Jesus Christ.

Any other gospel that is not of the Lord is a false gospel and needs to be removed.

This is one of the foundational issues in the church today is that pastors have stopped guarding their gates, they have stopped keeping the false teachers out and instead they have welcomed them in because most of the time the false teachers have influence and money that the church enjoys receiving. There is no other gospel than that of Jesus Christ, and him crucified and anything and everything else must be rejected.

1:8 But though we, or an angel from heaven, preach any other gospel unto you than that which we have preached unto you, let him be accursed. Paul is including himself into this comment. He is simply saying that if anyone including them as the apostles preach or teach anything else other than what we already told you, and if any other message comes that is not focused on Jesus Christ than it is to be rejected and removed.

This is why in our churches today it is crucial to determine that you believe the bible to be true for what it says. There are many different versions out today, and since God said that he would preserve his perfect inspired word to all generations than there must be one perfect version and that my reader friend is the King James version[1].

This is not the time or place for a bible version discussion however it is the perfect time to say that we must get that perfect version, read it, study it, learn it, live by it, and that my dear reader friend will grow ones faith in the Lord and then the false doctrines will not be allowed to come in. The bible tells us that our faith comes from the word of God so if we are in the word our faith increases as well as our convictions and passions for the gospel.

1:9 As we said before, so say I now again, If any man preach any other gospel unto you than that ye have received, let him be accursed. Accursed simply defined is: *being under a curse*. Paul is telling this church here that the people that are spreading this lie, this false doctrine, that they are under a curse from God. Paul says to let them be under that curse.

When someone, anyone who comes in and tears down what the Lord has established, they will

[1] See the authors book "The KJV is for Me: why I use the King James Bible"

deal directly with God himself, as he is God, and he has to punish sin. Remember the bible tells us that everyone of us, you, me, and the fat lady in the choir all must stand before God one day, alone, and in his sight and have to answer for what we have done or taught others on this earth.

I often say or share with people in our church is that one of my biggest fears in the Lord is that I will preach or teach something that is not in line with the bible, something that is not truth and will as a result of that lead people in the wrong path and have to answer to God himself for that. I pray that never happens and as long as I continue in the word, and guard my gates and build my walls[2] as the bible tells us to, I will not fall in this area.

1:10 For do I now persuade men, or God? or do I seek to please men? for if I yet pleased men, I should not be the servant of Christ.
Paul is making it clear here that allowing a false doctrine in, by allowing anything that is not of the Lord that they no longer serve the Lord, but they are now serving man.

---

[2] See the authors book "Unguarded Gates: The Local church" for a detailed study on guarding gates in your life

All false religions, each, and every one of them, will put the glory and power on man and remove it from the Lord.

Salvation only through Jesus Christ as the bible tells us, places all authority and power on Jesus Christ, salvation by doing good, by killing infidels, by living a good life puts all power and glory on man and removes it from the Lord.

I will most likely make someone upset with me here, but any and all other beliefs that are not in line with the bible, not the nonexistent "original manuscripts", but the bible itself removes all authority and power from the Lord Jesus Christ and places it on sinful man.

1:11 But I certify you, brethren, that the gospel which was preached of me is not after man. Paul is telling them that he is preaching the truth, that he received his message from the Lord and not from man-made religions. Don't forget Paul was against Christianity and the things of the Lord, when he was Saul, he was persecuting and killing Christians he hated the message of the gospel, so if any man had the proof of the Lord, it was this man Paul that had it as he was transformed to a new man in Christ just as we are once we are saved. Paul tells this church here that his messages of the gospel is not after sinful man, but it is from a sinless Savior.

1:12 For I neither received it of man, neither was I taught it, but by the revelation of Jesus Christ. Paul is very clear here to make it known that the gospel he preached and taught and the scriptures that he used as guides to establish churches was not from man, or any of man's knowledge, but that it was revealed to him by Jesus Christ.

1:13 For ye have heard of my conversation in time past in the Jews' religion, how that beyond measure I persecuted the church of God, and wasted it: Paul is reminding them of how he has told them his testimony of how he was a persecutor of the church of God. How he had killed and imprisoned Christians and their families. Paul is using the experience of his life to highlight the false doctrine that this church bought into and how any doctrine that is not of the bible will lead you away from Jesus Christ.

1:14 And profited in the Jews' religion above many my equals in mine own nation, being more exceedingly zealous of the traditions of my fathers. Paul was a well-known among the

Jews and a man with a high status among them. He was a man that people looked up to, when he was in this false religion, he set the example for others in many cases, for them to persecute the church as well. Paul was a rough man, a man with no compassion, or love for others at that time.

No compassion and no love for others are fruits of evilness. Fruits of evilness will be revealed in any person that is not seeking God. A true believer in Jesus Christ will love the unlovable, they will tell anyone and everyone about the saving knowledge of Jesus Christ, they will not hate certain people and only love others. Many other false religions will only love certain people while at the same time hating others.

1:15 But when it pleased God, who separated me from my mother's womb, and called me by his grace, Paul is identifying that it is God that gives people the talents and abilities they need for his service, and he gives them to these people from the time they are created in the mother's womb.

God will always make sure that people have what they need for the work they are set aside to do, and most of the time these people do not even know they have these gifts until they begin to serve the Lord.

As an example, growing up I hated, I mean absolutely hated reading and writing and never felt the need to do anything ever with it except to be able to read to understand certain things as they would come up in life.

Little did I know the Lord orchestrated my entire education system from elementary school through high school to be a school based on reading and comprehension. I had no teacher in front of my class teaching, no, our school was the A.C.E. system which consists of workbooks that you must read and write and answer questions from. I Had reluctantly accomplished this all through school and graduated. While in my teen age years I had surrendered to preach, at that time I felt it was in the area of being a missionary, however the Lord had me pastoring.

So after high school I started the whole Bible college thing which was also the same type of system that my grade schooling was. At that time, I did not see the Lord was preparing me for his ministry by developing in me some of the gifts he has given me by my writing which I do and value now, as for me my writings are studies and a great way to learn the bible. Folks, this is what God does.

1:16 To reveal his Son in me, that I might preach him among the heathen; immediately I conferred not with flesh and blood: Paul said that when the Lord had called him to preach to the unloved, the heathen, the Gentiles, he did not go and seek man's advice, or man's approval, he did not reason within himself he just went and did as the Lord instructed him to do.

1:17 Neither went I up to Jerusalem to them which were apostles before me; but I went into Arabia, and returned again unto Damascus. When one confers with the flesh and with them that are not seeking God, usually they will be given false advice, and advice that is not in line with the service of the Lord. Paul is saying here that he did not talk himself out of this, once the Lord told him what he was to do, and he was surrendered to do it, he just went and did it.

My dear reader friend, it is all about you being fully surrendered to the Lord for him to be able to work through you, yes that fully surrendered might mean that you walk away from that hundred-thousand dollar a year job and live on faith, yes that might mean that you go from a mansion in Beverley hills to a cabin in the woods in back woods Africa.

All the stuff on the earth stays on the earth when you die, you still die, not one single thing goes with you, you end up in one of the same two place I end up, for me it is eternity with Jesus because I am a saved born-again child of God, if you are not, you will burn and be tormented for all eternity without Jesus Christ.

1:18 Then after three years I went up to Jerusalem to see Peter, and abode with him fifteen days. Paul had his three years of learning the bible, working with others in the ministry, and getting ready to go and do. After this time was over he went to be with Peter for about two weeks and then went on his journeys to share the gospel and plant churches so the word of God can multiply.

1:19 But other of the apostles saw I none, save James the Lord's brother. Paul did not see the other apostles. This is an important comment as Paul is reminding this church here that his education, his understanding of the scripture and the things of God was not from man as he did not really have that opportunity to be influenced by man, he was taught by God through only one man for the three years and that is all part of the authority that he claims to have in the Lord. Praise the Lord, folks, we can have that same kind of training from the Lord himself by just simply believing the bible for what it says without question, and you will see what God will do with you.

1:20 Now the things which I write unto you, behold, before God, I lie not. Paul is basically saying “I swear to God I am telling you the truth” all that he is writing is based on truth and that he promises on the name of God (so to speak) that he is telling them the truth.

1:21 Afterwards I came into the regions of Syria and Cilicia; These are the cities that Paul went to after he had left Peter after those two weeks with him.

1:22 And was unknown by face unto the churches of Judaea which were in Christ: Here we see that there were some churches already established in the name of Christ. The local church did not start with Paul but by the Lord Jesus Christ as he is the rock that the churches are built on.

Paul was unknown to these churches and Just as Paul was taught by the Lord there were other men at that time that had been taught by godly men and they planted churches as well, Paul and Peter are just the ones that the Lord used and highlighted to get salvation known to others.

In every society, and in every generation, there will be those for the Lord that are well known by others. I think in our generation of men like Jack Hyles, Billy Graham, Lester Roloff, Peter Rockman, and others. These men were known for their love and dedication for the Lord, they were used greatly by God to get the message of salvation out to the lost world.

There were also many Pastor John Does out there that were preaching and teaching the same message that almost no one has heard about in the world today, however their impact was so great for the cause of the Lord that for some of them the fruit of their ministries are still going.

Paul was one of those that God had highlighted to do his work, God had placed Paul and Peter in the public spotlight while the other apostles were doing the same thing, however you do not hear much about them, God was still with them, he still loved them, God walked with them in the difficult times and was a comforter to them in the hurting times but God was still God and he used each person for his service that was needed to be used for.

1:23 But they had heard only, That he which persecuted us in times past now preacheth the faith which once he destroyed. These churches that did not know Paul, had only heard of him when he was in the public spotlight for destroying the church and now, they love and support him. Not because they changed their belief or doctrine, but because the Lord had changed the apostle Paul and he was now a Christian on fire for Jesus Christ.

1:24 And they glorified God in me. These churches are now glorifying God. They are supporting Paul; they are no longer afraid of him. This should serve as a testimony to others how since these churches were against and afraid of Paul for his persecution of them, and now they are supporting him that the Lord has saved and called Paul and separated him unto the ministry. This gives more authority to Paul and his writings to this church to get them back on track for him.

CHAPTER TWO

Galatians 2:1-21
Then fourteen years after I went up again to Jerusalem with Barnabas, and took Titus with me also. And I went up by revelation, and communicated unto them that gospel which I preach among the Gentiles, but privately to them which were of reputation, lest by any means I should run, or had run, in vain. But neither Titus, who was with me, being a Greek, was compelled to be circumcised: And that because of false brethren unawares brought in, who came in privily to spy out our liberty which we have in Christ Jesus, that they might bring us into bondage: To whom we gave place by subjection, no, not for an hour; that the truth of the gospel might continue with you. But of these who seemed to be somewhat, (whatsoever they were, it maketh no matter to me: God accepteth no man's person:) for they who seemed to be somewhat in conference added nothing to me: But contrariwise, when they saw that the gospel of the uncircumcision was committed unto me, as the gospel of the circumcision was unto Peter; (For he that wrought effectually in Peter to the apostleship of the circumcision, the same was mighty in me toward the

Gentiles:) And when James, Cephas, and John, who seemed to be pillars, perceived the grace that was given unto me, they gave to me and Barnabas the right hands of fellowship; that we should go unto the heathen, and they unto the circumcision. Only they would that we should remember the poor; the same which I also was forward to do. But when Peter was come to Antioch, I withstood him to the face, because he was to be blamed. For before that certain came from James, he did eat with the Gentiles: but when they were come, he withdrew and separated himself, fearing them which were of the circumcision. And the other Jews dissembled likewise with him; insomuch that Barnabas also was carried away with their dissimulation. But when I saw that they walked not uprightly according to the truth of the gospel, I said unto Peter before them all, If thou, being a Jew, livest after the manner of Gentiles, and not as do the Jews, why compellest thou the Gentiles to live as do the Jews? We who are Jews by nature, and not sinners of the Gentiles, Knowing that a man is not justified by the works of the law, but by the faith of Jesus Christ, even we have believed in Jesus Christ, that we might be justified by the faith of Christ, and not by the

works of the law: for by the works of the law shall no flesh be justified. But if, while we seek to be justified by Christ, we ourselves also are found sinners, is therefore Christ the minister of sin? God forbid. For if I build again the things which I destroyed, I make myself a transgressor. For I through the law am dead to the law, that I might live unto God. I am crucified with Christ: nevertheless I live; yet not I, but Christ liveth in me: and the life which I now live in the flesh I live by the faith of the Son of God, who loved me, and gave himself for me. I do not frustrate the grace of God: for if righteousness come by the law, then Christ is dead in vain.

COMMENTARY

2:1 Then fourteen years after I went up again to Jerusalem with Barnabas, and took Titus with me also. Paul is telling the folks in this church how he has been faithful in his presentation of the gospel; he has been very careful to make sure that it is God that gets the glory for the message of the gospel and that Paul was not doing any of this for his own gain. All false gospels and doctrines are for man's gain and not the Lords.

2:2 And I went up by revelation, and communicated unto them that gospel which I preach among the Gentiles, but privately to them which were of reputation, lest by any means I should run, or had run, in vain. Paul went to these churches in Judea by a revelation form the Lord and went to preach the gospel to the Gentiles. This is the same thing that you or I may have if we believe that the Lord is leading us to go somewhere and do ministry there, that we go and we let him work out all the details. This would be, how we say, the Lord told us to do this, that is the same thing as a revelation that is being talked about here.

2:3 But neither Titus, who was with me, being a Greek, was compelled to be circumcised: Titus was a Gentile that was converted to a Christian. Part of the Old Testament was that the people of the Lord had to be circumcised. Yes, the same circumcision that we see today, but in the New Testament, salvation was for all that believed, and circumcision was no longer a requirement to be a child of God. Titus did not get circumcised, though he was a Greek (Gentile) and he was a helper for Paul a spreader of the gospel. Titus actually has a book of the bible that Paul wrote to him on keeping guard in the local church and watching for the enemy to come in an devour.

2:4 And that because of false brethren unawares brought in, who came in privily to spy out our liberty which we have in Christ Jesus, that they might bring us into bondage: There were people in the church that were still of the belief that one must be circumcised to a child of God, and they are spreading and teaching this false doctrine.

Privily simply defined is: *to do in secret*. These false Christians (brethren) came into the group with bad intentions but they came in under the premise of being one of the believers and supporters and I'm sure they were trying to get people on their side so they can shut down the message of the gospel.

People do this all the time. Instead of them repenting of the wrongs they have done, instead of them wanting what God wants for them, they resist, they rebel, and they try to tear down the things of God and the people that God is using so they can feel good about themselves, and their pride is not hurt then. They so forget that we will all stand before the God of the bible individually and have to answer for our actions in the Lord what we did for him or what we did against him.

These false brethren were wanting to catch Paul and Titus up in a false gospel and get them shamed so the people would reject them. If you are doing things for yourself you will get into bondage in your life, if you are doing things for the Lord he will deliver you and walk with you through the testing and the trials.

2:5 To whom we gave place by subjection, no, not for an hour; that the truth of the gospel might continue with you. This verse seems to be a little confusing on the surface. The first time I read it, it seemed as if Paul let these false teachers have time to speak but only a short time and not for an hour or longer.

I'm confident that I am not the only one that read it that way, however, is what this verse is actually saying is that not for any amount of time, not even an hour did Paul subject (cause) these false teachers to speak or teach, he did not give them subjection to do so because he did not want the new or soon to be new converts getting confused and having a false understanding of the things of God.

This my dear friend is what the churches must do today is to protect the church and the flock of the church to only hear the truth of the bible. Paul was making sure these brethren were only hearing the truth.

When a person has read, learned, and understands the truth of the Lord and the bible all false beliefs and doctrines will be spotted and that person that spots them will take the necessary steps to protect the truth. This is why my dear reader friend it is crucial that you and I are in the bible every day, that we are following the guidelines in the bible and that we are seeking God with all our hearts, minds, and souls to keep us on the right path.

2:6 But of these who seemed to be somewhat, (whatsoever they were, it maketh no matter to me: God accepteth no man's person:) for they who seemed to be somewhat in conference added nothing to me: Those that seemed to be somewhat were those that seemed like they were the knowledgeable ones, they were the smart ones of the group. In any conversation with religious people there is always one that does most of the talking and one that does most of the listening. The one that does most of the talking is the one that seems to be “the somewhat” that is being referred to here. Somewhat simply defined is: *something*. These people felt they were something, but Paul says they were of no value to him.

Paul goes on to say that God accepts no man’s person. This is confirming another verse or two in the bible that says that God has NO respect of persons (Romans 2:11, Acts 10:34) this does not mean that God is disrespectful, it simply means that God does not play favorites, he does not treat others better than he treats others as that would make him an unfair God. God does not treat the person that tithes more better than the person that does not tithe at all, he treats and loves each and every person the same.

To simplify what Paul is saying here is that these people, these false prophets, that Paul gave no time for them to talk, when he was in conversation with them, they were of no value to him, and they were not as important as they felt they were.

2:7 But contrariwise, when they saw that the gospel of the uncircumcision was committed unto me, as the gospel of the circumcision was unto Peter; The gospel of the circumcision was simply that those that believed in God became his children, and that was shown by them getting circumcised. This was initially intended for one race of people that was God's race, however once Jesus Christ came to pay for the sins of the world this gospel was now for everyone both the Jew and the Gentile, both the circumcised and the uncircumcised. Circumcision is NO longer a requirement for salvation.

Peter had the task of spreading the gospel to the Jews, this was a difficult task in itself as Peter seemed at times to not like the Gentiles. It was in a vision in the book of Acts that Peter had from the Lord that told him that his salvation was also for the Gentiles just as it was for the Jews. This has been a very hard concept for the people of these times to accept. Paul was given the task of spreading the gospel to the Gentiles. It would take someone with a tough outer shell to take on this task and the Lord said that would be the apostle, Paul.

2:8 (For he that wrought effectually in Peter to the apostleship of the circumcision, the same was mighty in me toward the Gentiles:) Simply put Paul is saying that the same God of the bible gave both Paul and Peter their messages and their missions, they were both to spread the gospel, one was to go to the Jews the other was to the Gentiles. One to the religious (lost) people (Jews) one to the Gentiles (lost) but both having the same gospel message.

2:9 And when James, Cephas, and John, who seemed to be pillars, perceived the grace that was given unto me, they gave to me and Barnabas the right hands of fellowship; that we should go unto the heathen, and they unto the circumcision. These men James, Cephas, and John were men of integrity, they were known among the people, among the towns, they were well established in the communities and in the faith that wen they said something people listened to them, their word was gold and they could be trusted. People who have this kind of a reputation, are people who are careful to recommend things to others, or certain books and what not.

These men of respect, they gave their blessing and approval to Paul and Barnabas to go and do what the Lord had told them to do. In other words, they were given blessings to go and do and that they would be a supporter of them. This would be the same as we see in the book of Nehemiah, how he had a burden to build the wall and the king let him go and build. Not only did the king let Nehemiah go and build he gave him his approval in letters for all the supplies he needed, for free passages, and his army to go with Nehemiah this showed support from the king. This is the same with these men here they gave their support to Paul and Barnabas.

2:10 Only they would that we should remember the poor; the same which I also was forward to do. Paul says that these men of respect gave him their blessing with the only added benefit that they had encouraged Paul and Barnabas to remember the poor.

Paul says that he did remember the poor and helped them as much as he could. We should still do this in our society today, but be careful when it comes to the poor to make sure they are poor, and let me let you in on a little secret my dear reader friend just because a person is homeless does not mean they are poor, if they can work and choose not to than that is part of the lifestyle they have chosen and not poor. Poor is those that have less than adequate food and clothes to live by, almost all homeless have plenty of food and clothes, I know because we work with them for three years.

2:11 But when Peter was come to Antioch, I withstood him to the face, because he was to be blamed. Paul is saying here that he and Peter had it out a little, that Paul rebuked Peter because Peter would not eat with the Gentiles, Peter was somewhat racist against him, and Paul was calling him out on that. If the gospel is also for the Gentiles and the Lord showed both Paul and Peter that it was, then Peter was to love the lost, he was to love the Gentiles and not refuse to be with them.

2:12 For before that certain came from James, he did eat with the Gentiles: but when they were come, he withdrew and separated himself, fearing them which were of the circumcision. Peter had some issues with stranding up for what he believes when the time for him to stand had come. Remember he denied Christ three times, now he ran from the Gentiles when the Jews showed up because he did not want to have the conflict. This is a lack of boldness ion Peter.

Many of us have a lack of boldness in our lives, I can absolutely assure you that when you are in the bible, your faith increases, and that faith being increased will also increase your boldness to tell others about the Lord and to stand strong when people are against you.

2:13 And the other Jews dissembled likewise with him; insomuch that Barnabas also was carried away with their dissimulation. Dissembled simply defined is: *to have a false appearance*. Peter and some of the jews had put on a false appearance and Peter was not willing to show the gospel in him to the Gentiles unless he could just do it in secret. Paul's traveling companion Barnabas was also caught up in this as well, when Peter and some of the other Christians had left the presence of the Gentiles, because they were too afraid to show their love for them in front of the Jews that he went with them and did the same thing.

2:14 But when I saw that they walked not uprightly according to the truth of the gospel, I said unto Peter before them all, If thou, being a Jew, livest after the manner of Gentiles, and not as do the Jews, why compellest thou the Gentiles to live as do the Jews? Paul had seen that these men were hypocrites, when it came to the spreading of the gospel that they would spread the gospel but would not live the gospel. In other words Peter and his group would tell the Gentiles to live a certain way but would not do that themselves, this is what is being said here. When Paul sees that this is what was happening he then asks Peter a question.

He asks Peter how can you tell the Gentiles that they need to live like the Jews but you yourself are not living like the Jews? How can we as Christians tell the lost world they need to get saved and go to church when we ourselves are not going to church either? how can we share the power of the bible to people when we are not having the power of the bible on our lives as well.

2:15 We who are Jews by nature, and not sinners of the Gentiles, Paul says that they were by birth Jews, that they were not born in the non-chosen race. They are all sinners, even the Jews were sinners, they were not automatically saved because they were Jews, just that the Jews were the only ones at that time that were believers of God, and outsiders that believed had to become Jews to show their salvation.

We are under grace now and grace has no boundaries on who is chosen by God and who is not, we are all predestined to be saved, but only those that receive the free gift of salvation will be the ones that get saved.

2:16 Knowing that a man is not justified by the works of the law, but by the faith of Jesus Christ, even we have believed in Jesus Christ, that we might be justified by the faith of Christ, and not by the works of the law: for by the works of the law shall no flesh be justified. This verse has a large impact in it. We see that it clearly says that no man, no person, past, present, or future can ever be good enough to get themselves into heaven. NO man is justified by the works of the law.

Paul then goes on to say that even him and Peter and some of the others have believed in Jesus Christ (that is the ONLY way to salvation) that they are justified by faith. It has always been faith that justified, Abraham and Enoch and many others in the bible only got to heaven by faith in the Lord Jesus Christ. I understand that Jesus had not come to the earth in the Old testament times, however the Old testament always speaks of the coming of a Savior and these folks would have to have a belief in God for their salvation which put them in Abraham's bosom when they died, sort of like a resting place, until the payment for sin could be made by Jesus Christ. It was only those that had faith in God that were spared from hell fire.

Then Paul finishes up this verse by simply saying that not one single good deed, or obedience to the law can ever save a person. Look at some of the laws today, our laws make murdering unborn babies legal, would that be accepted in God's eyes? You cannot rely on the ever-changing God rejecting laws that we have today, and the law that was in the Old Testament that was given to Moses was a moral law for the children of God to live by, to get the evilness of Egypt out of them, but it was not a saving law. We have the bible today for our moral law. The law in itself was not part of God's initial design, if there were never any sin, then there would never be a need for the law.

2:17 But if, while we seek to be justified by Christ, we ourselves also are found sinners, is therefore Christ the minister of sin? God forbid. Paul is telling this church here that if he is a child of God, a saved person, and lives in sin, or lives like the sinful world, does that mean then that Christ is the minister of sin? No he is not. Christ brings salvation and asks us as believers to live like him, like the bible tells us to live. When we live in sin, we do no good for the cause of Christ and we actually become a hindrance to the gospel of Jesus Christ. The bible tells us that this kind of living is called carnality (Romans 8:6-7)

2:18 For if I build again the things which I destroyed, I make myself a transgressor. Paul says that if he runs right back and jumps back into his sin that he was saved from he makes himself a transgressor. He will have to answer to God for his actions. He will not lose his salvation as that is impossible to do (Ephesians 4:30) but he will bring God's judgment upon himself because he is building that sinful life that Jesus Christ died to free him from.

My dear reader friend this is still true today for you and I, we can run back to our sinful ways and rebuild that sin that we were living in, however we will suffer the condemnation of that sin here on this earth, we will not lose our salvation, but we will have to answer to God. Praise God for his forgiveness and washing away of our sins so we can be restored back to him (I John 1:9)

2:19 For I through the law am dead to the law, that I might live unto God. Paul as a saved person is no longer under the law, as it is not the law that saves but Christ that saves, the law can only send a person to the lake of fire for all eternity. Paul says that he is dead to that law, he is saved so now he is alive unto God. It is now his responsibility to live for God.

2:20 I am crucified with Christ: nevertheless I live; yet not I, but Christ liveth in me: and the life which I now live in the flesh I live by the faith of the Son of God, who loved me, and gave himself for me. Our old sin nature is crucified with Christ, when Christ went to the cross, he took the payment for yours, mine, and all the world's sin with him, once that payment is applied to us through salvation, we are a new person in Christ Jesus. The old sinful desires are gone, we will still sin, we will still have those temptations, I can tell you from experience in my own life, that if you are not intentional about walking with God, you will give into those temptations and go the carnal way for quite a while.[3] Yes we will sin at times and the Holy Spirit will convict us of that sin, we live our lives

---

[3] See the authors work "redemption: a true-Life Prodigal" it is his life story

by faith in Jesus Christ, that my friend is what gets us through this life and living in this evil sinful wickedness of this beautiful world that God created.

2:21 I do not frustrate the grace of God: for if righteousness come by the law, then Christ is dead in vain. Paul is saying that he is not wanting to be a hindrance to the gospel, that if it was good deeds that saved a person than it was useless for Christ to have died on the cross, it was in vain and necessary. Each and every other doctrine makes the crucifixion not necessary, including those that believed that God chose some for heaven and some for hell.

If God had already predestined some for hell and some for heaven then Calvary was just in vain as it was not need because the grace of God has already been applied to that chosen person, they are going to heaven no matter what they do, as the one chosen for hell is already going to hell no matter how much they may want to get saved. Each and every belief that is not in line with the bible rejects Jesus' death on the cross.

CHAPTER THREE

Galatians 3:1-29

O foolish Galatians, who hath bewitched you, that ye should not obey the truth, before whose eyes Jesus Christ hath been evidently set forth, crucified among you? This only would I learn of you, Received ye the Spirit by the works of the law, or by the hearing of faith? Are ye so foolish? having begun in the Spirit, are ye now made perfect by the flesh? Have ye suffered so many things in vain? if it be yet in vain. He therefore that ministereth to you the Spirit, and worketh miracles among you, doeth he it by the works of the law, or by the hearing of faith? Even as

Abraham believed God, and it was accounted to him for righteousness. Know ye therefore that they which are of faith, the same are the children of Abraham. And the scripture, foreseeing that God would justify the heathen through faith, preached before the gospel unto Abraham, saying, In thee shall all nations be blessed. So then they which be of faith are blessed with faithful Abraham. For as many as are of the works of the law are under the curse: for it is written, Cursed is every one that continueth not in all things which are written in the book of the law to do them. But that no man is justified by the law in the sight of God, it is evident: for, The just shall live by faith. And the law is not of faith: but, The man that doeth them shall live in them. Christ hath redeemed us from the curse of the law, being made a curse for us: for it is written, Cursed is every one that hangeth on a tree: That the blessing of Abraham might come on the Gentiles through Jesus Christ; that we might receive the promise of the Spirit through faith. Brethren, I speak after the manner of men; Though it be but a man's covenant, yet if it be confirmed, no man disannulleth, or addeth thereto. Now to Abraham and his seed were the promises made. He saith not, And to seeds, as of many; but as of one, And to thy seed, which is Christ. And this I say, that the covenant, that was confirmed before of God in Christ, the law, which was four hundred and thirty years after, cannot disannul, that it should make the promise of none effect. For if the inheritance be of the law, it is no more of promise: but God gave it to Abraham by promise. Wherefore then serveth the law? It was added because of transgressions, till the seed should come to whom the promise was made; and it was ordained by angels in the hand of a mediator. Now a mediator is not a mediator of one, but God is one. Is the law then against the promises of God? God forbid: for if there had been a law given which could have given life, verily righteousness should have been by the law. But the scripture hath concluded all under sin, that the promise by faith of Jesus Christ might be given to them that believe. But before faith came, we were kept under the law, shut up unto the faith which should afterwards be revealed. Wherefore the law was our schoolmaster to bring us unto Christ, that we might be justified by faith. But after that faith is come, we are no longer under a schoolmaster. For ye are all the children of God by faith in Christ Jesus. For

as many of you as have been baptized into Christ have put on Christ. There is neither Jew nor Greek, there is neither bond nor free, there is neither male nor female: for ye are all one in Christ Jesus. And if ye be Christ's, then are ye Abraham's seed, and heirs according to the promise.

COMMENTARY

3:1 O foolish Galatians, who hath bewitched you, that ye should not obey the truth, before whose eyes Jesus Christ hath been evidently set forth, crucified among you? Bewitched simply defined is: *to control or affect as by a magical spell*. Paul is asking the folks in this church who has come in and influenced them to leave the faith that they were once with. It had to be someone that came in and told them things that were not so. Yes these saints here did not have the completed bible that we have today, however they did have some scriptures, they had the faith in the Lord, and they let that faith get diverted and perverted by false doctrines and false prophets that entered into the church.

This still happen today as well, it is crucial that we as Christians keep in the bible so our faith can increase, our convictions for our faith can strengthen, and we can remove and eliminate any false doctrines that come through our doors. Paul uses the word “obey” here, saying, that these people chose not to obey the truth that they knew that Jesus Christ was crucified, there were some in that group that were there at the crucifixion we know this by the phrase that “among you”

3:2 This only would I learn of you, Received ye the Spirit by the works of the law, or by the hearing of faith? Paul is asking the saints here at this church if they had received the Holy Spirit by faith or by works, he knows, and they know that the Holy Spirit only comes in by faith in the Lord Jesus Christ.

3:3 Are ye so foolish? having begun in the Spirit, are ye now made perfect by the flesh? Paul is asking the saints here if they are so foolish to believe that they began their walk in the Lord by faith and the Holy Spirit living in them, that all of a sudden they now walk in the Lord by works only, by the deeds of the law. All man-made religions will lead you to works instead of faith for salvation. These folks had diverted from the faith and were convinced they had to follow the law to be righteous in the sight of God. Paul was calling them out on this as they knew better.

3:4 Have ye suffered so many things in vain? if it be yet in vain. Paul is simply asking the saints here that all the persecution that they have suffered as all Christian churches back then did and many today still do, did they suffer through all that in vain or did they suffer through it because of faith? it was the faith that made them strong, it was faith that gave them the strength to endure it was not based on any deeds of the law that they are now being convinced to follow.

3:5 He therefore that ministereth to you the Spirit, and worketh miracles among you, doeth he it by the works of the law, or by the hearing of faith? The saints here are being asked if all that the Lord has done for them, the healings, the miracles, etc., were they all done by the works of the law? It would be impossible, as the law can only judge a person and can never heal a person. All this that was being done was by faith and the Holy Spirit working in the believers.

People today want to live by the law and not by faith, the reason for this is because the law judges people, and if you are in the law you can be judge of others to point out all their mistakes and sins, while at the same time ignoring your own sins. This is common among people and among believers, we love to judge others, we all know those bible verses that support our judging of others while at the same time we ignore the verses in the bible that tell us that we are to be judged by that same judgment and that we are to judge ourselves first.

3:6 Even as Abraham believed God, and it was accounted to him for righteousness. Abraham believe God, he had faith in the Lord. Remember the time when the Lord asked him to sacrifice his only son on that alter? Abraham knew that God would make a provision for the sacrifice, he knew that if indeed he had to kill his son that God would raise him from the dead, we know this because God told him that his son would be the blood line for God's people. Abraham had enough faith to trust God at that moment without knowing when or how that sacrificial animal would be provided. This is what is lacking in our churches today, is faith that the Lord will do what he says he will do.

Abrahams faith made him a righteous man, it made him a man that walked with God, it made him a man that showed that he loved God and that he would obey what the Lord told him to do. We need more Abrahams in our societies today, we need men and women that will have the faith in the Lord when they cannot see anything in front of them, we need people today who will trust God and walk in the way that they should walk so God can use us to accomplish his work.

3:7 Know ye therefore that they which are of faith, the same are the children of Abraham. The Christians that have accepted the Lord Jesus Christ as their personal Savior are of that bloodline of Abraham, they are children of Abraham. There is a children's song out that simply says "Father Abraham had many sons" you should google it and listen to it, it is a cute little song with a powerful impact, the entire point of this song and this verse is that when a person gets saved, they become part of Abrahams seed.

3:8 And the scripture, foreseeing that God would justify the heathen through faith, preached before the gospel unto Abraham, saying, In thee shall all nations be blessed. The Holy scriptures taught that Abraham would be the father of many nations, that all his seed, his bloodline would be blessed. Abraham was not blessed because he kept the law, or because he was a nice guy, he was blessed because he loved the Lord, he had FAITH in what the Lord told him, he believed the scriptures for what they said, and you know what my dear friend, the scriptures were right.

I have a question for you the reader, if the scriptures were right back then and no believers questioned them and they were proven true, then why do “believers” doubt them today? It is because of a lack of faith.

3:9 So then they which be of faith are blessed with faithful Abraham. Just as God blessed and protected Abraham, so will he for all who are believers. Yes, you may have difficult times ahead, yes there will be pain for you at times in the things of the Lord, but the Lord will walk side by side and most of the time ahead of you so you can get through whatever it is by his grace and love and the peace that faith in the Lord brings

3:10 For as many as are of the works of the law are under the curse: for it is written, Cursed is every one that continueth not in all things which are written in the book of the law to do them. Paul is pointing out to the saints here that the law is only going to lead people to hell, the law was designed to judge sin and sinful behavior, it in no way makes any person, past, present, or future righteous.

The law cannot save, the law puts people under bondage, the law is a curse so in essence Paul is asking these people why are you following after a curse when you are freed from that cure by the Lord.

The only way for any person to ever be considered righteous by the law is for that person to have never ever broken even one little iota of the law, not one bad thought, not one bad reaction to a situation, not one thing. The only person I know that could do that was Jesus Christ.

3:11 But that no man is justified by the law in the sight of God, it is evident: for, The just shall live by faith. The law as I stated in previous verses was designed to judge sin. It is not a saving law, the only way for a person to be saved is through faith in the Lord Jesus Christ. Notice here also it is not just a saving faith that the believers must have but it is also a living faith. If you believe that Jesus Christ died for your sins on the cross and that he saved you from the lake of fire you must live by that belief. We as Christians must live by faith.

We must have faith in the bible as the truth of the word of God, we must have faith in what the bible says and believe it and live it for what it says. This verse here says that it is evident, it is proof, that the law cannot save anyone at any time, yet the world then and especially now believes that is in "through themselves", through keeping the law, through their own works, that they can get saved.

3:12 And the law is not of faith: but, The man that doeth them shall live in them. The law is NOT faith. we can see the law, we can do our best to keep the law we will all at times break the law, and yes my dear reader friend you have broken the law and since you have broken the law you are going to burn in a lake of fire for all eternity.

You may say I don't break the law, ok take driving for an example, there have been times that you have gone over the speed limit, even one single mile over the speed limit is breaking that law, just because you did not get a ticket does not mean that you did not break that law. You are guilty.

I praise the Lord that through faith there is also forgiveness and restoration.(I John 1:9) That not only does God forgive us he also cleanses us, washes us white as snow, we become clean through him and faith in him. Faith in the Lord comes from the word of God.

If we can see what we are doing then it is not faith. Faith is believing in something that you cannot see but you know it is there. You have faith that when you plug in your cell phone that the electricity will be there in that outlet, so you plug in your phone knowing that and that faith is made whole once that phone shows it is charging. We have faith that Jesus died on the cross for us, we do not see Jesus, but we know he lives because we have received him into our hearts, we are his child, our faith is strengthened when we plug ourselves into the outlet, which is the bible and once that charging takes place, we can at the end see that faith, we see our faith once we see Jesus. We must live by faith, living by sight is only a man-made religion.

Paul is telling this church here that yes we can see the law, we know what the law is, but all we can do is our best to keep that law. Doing ones best is not being perfect at it, doing your best means you made the least amount of mistakes that you could and were close to keeping it, but you still were not perfect at it. The bible tells us that if any person breaks the smallest little law that he is guilty of breaking them all. (James 2:10)

3:13 Christ hath redeemed us from the curse of the law, being made a curse for us: for it is written, Cursed is every one that hangeth on a tree: Jesus Christ came to this earth for one reason and that was to take that sin debt from you and I. The bible says that everyone that hangs on a tree, everyone that is crucified is cursed, they have done the vilest of wrongs and are sentenced to death. Jesus was not an evil man, he did no wrong as he was perfect, it was a perfect person that had the power to pay the sin debt for the world. Jesus took that sin debt, he took that punishment that you and I so deserved, and he became a cursed man for us. Oh what a Saviour, oh hallelujah he gave his life for you and I. Paul is telling this church here that Jesus did just that for them.

3:14 That the blessing of Abraham might come on the Gentiles through Jesus Christ; that we might receive the promise of the Spirit through faith. Paul is reminding this church here that through Jesus Christ is how salvation came to the Gentiles. In the bible there are basically two types of people, Jews initially God's chosen people, and Gentiles, which is everyone else. Because of Christ dying on that cross for our sins the blessing that was given to Abraham and his seed, is now extended to any and all who believe on Jesus Christ, it is no longer under the law as the law cannot save it never has and never will. Praise God for the age of grace as to which we live in.

3:15 Brethren, I speak after the manner of men; Though it be but a man's covenant, yet if it be confirmed, no man disannulleth, or addeth thereto. Paul is relating the blessing that was Abraham and that it is now for the Gentiles as well like a covenant made by man. That covenant has been made, it is sealed, and no man can take away from it or add to it. It is a done deal.

We just came off of resurrection Sunday here in twenty twenty-two and we remember how on the cross Jesus said IT IS FINISHED, that is how this covenant is, it cannot be changed, or removed.

3:16 Now to Abraham and his seed were the promises made. He saith not, And to seeds, as of many; but as of one, And to thy seed, which is Christ. This Promise that was to Abraham was made not to the individual seeds, but to the collective seeds. The word seeds here, yes it is individual seeds, but as a whole, all of them together become the seeds of Abraham.

This is used as an example of salvation, the promise was made to the seed of Abraham, yes the collective seed as all people together, yet it saves each one individually. Any and all who get saved become part of that one collective seed. Just as we use the terms today the church, the body of Christ. Yes individual members who are saved, all are saved together in one body for Christ Jesus.

3:17 And this I say, that the covenant, that was confirmed before of God in Christ, the law, which was four hundred and thirty years after, cannot disannul, that it should make the promise of none effect. Yes the law was important, and it was the basis for all that people were to live by, it was what everyone knew, that as important and powerful as the law is, it could not remove, destroy, or make null and void the promise of God to bless the seed of Abraham, which in turn is salvation for all that receive that free gift. There is nothing, not one thing, that can make salvation of non-affect.

3:18 For if the inheritance be of the law, it is no more of promise: but God gave it to

Abraham by promise. If the law was the judge of salvation then it could not be a promise, because those who interpret the law, those who enforce the law are sinful human beings who make mistakes and they can then decide who would go to heaven and who would not, oh what a mess salvation would be in if it were left up to man to decide who went and who did not go. Salvation is given to us by God because he loves us.

3:19 Wherefore then serveth the law? It was added because of transgressions, till the seed should come to whom the promise was made; and it was ordained by angels in the hand of a mediator. The whole reason for the law was because of sin. if Adam had never sinned in the garden then we would never had known law. The law was around to guide people on how to live peaceably and morally but even with the law salvation was still by faith, in the Old Testament, salvation was still by faith. The law cannot then, or now ever get one single person into heaven. Salvation is only through Jesus Christ. (John 14:6)

3:20 Now a mediator is not a mediator of one, but God is one. It was God who was the mediator for salvation, it was God that had his son die on that cross, it was God that loved us enough. The bible tells us that Jesus becomes the mediator, not for salvation, but for man, Jesus is salvation, but he goes to God and pays for our sins which makes him a mediator for us. (I Timothy 2:5)

3:21 Is the law then against the promises of God? God forbid: for if there had been a law given which could have given life, verily righteousness should have been by the law. Again, Paul is reminding this church that law cannot go against salvation, the law cannot save any person, salvation is NOT by works, but by faith.

If the law could save, then anyone who kept the law would be sent to heaven. All people would have to do is to keep the law, which it is impossible for any person to keep all the laws they ever come across.

3:22 But the scripture hath concluded all under sin, that the promise by faith of Jesus Christ might be given to them that believe. Paul does here what I love doing and that is put the authority back on scripture, the bible is the final authority and that is what Paul is putting the authority on by saying, “the scripture hath concluded”

The promise of God to bless the seed of Abraham through salvation is for any and all people who trust in Jesus Christ. It is for the richest man in the world, it is for the poorest man in the world, it is for the man on death row and the man in the white house, salvation is for the drunkard on the street and the prostitute in the back alley it is for anyone and everyone that believes.

3:23 But before faith came, we were kept under the law, shut up unto the faith which should afterwards be revealed. Before Jesus Christ came salvation was by faith, but that message was not spread to the world, people had to follow the law, not to be saved, but to walk with God as they should, by keeping the law it provided some morality to them. If you want to see the simplest proof that salvation in the Old testament was by faith as it is today just go to Hebrews chapter eleven, it is referred to as the hall of faith.

The faith for salvation was only promoted in the children of Israel and to all who joined them, other than that the message was not revealed or available to the world until Jesus went to the cross.

3:24 Wherefore the law was our schoolmaster to bring us unto Christ, that we might be justified by faith. The law was the teacher of how to live for God just as the bible is today. Keeping the law allowed a person to have, or exercise that faith in God, the law was the guide to God. The bible today is the same anyone and everyone can receive it, they can read it but that does not mean that they will get saved, but it lets them know how to.

3:25 But after that faith is come, we are no longer under a schoolmaster. We are no longer under the law to get to salvation; we are under Christ as he is the one that paid that sin debt for us. Just as the law led to faith now Christ leads to faith.

3:26 For ye are all the children of God by faith in Christ Jesus. Once a person receives that gift of salvation they become a child of God no matter who they are or where they are from. It is by faith and faith alone that saved (Ephesians 2:8-9)

3:27 For as many of you as have been baptized into Christ have put on Christ. Those that have been baptized have shown that they are walking with Christ, they have also been baptized by the Holy Spirit unto salvation which is what guides them on how to live for Christ while they are here on this earth.

The Holy Spirit is what allows a Christian to put on that armour of God, it allows the Christian to walk in the faith of the Lord and to live our lives reflecting Jesus Christ.

Please note, water baptism is not required for salvation, but the Lord does tell us to get baptized as a symbol of his death, burial, and resurrection, it shows the washing away for the sinful man and the new man in Christ coming out and living for him.

3:28 There is neither Jew nor Greek, there is neither bond nor free, there is neither male nor female: for ye are all one in Christ Jesus. There are no restrictions on who can become a child of God it's for "whosoever" that calls on the name of the Lord that is who gets saved. (Romans 10:13)

3:29 And if ye be Christ's, then are ye Abraham's seed, and heirs according to the promise. Becoming a child of God through salvation in him, by you having faith in the Lord, you are automatically part of that seed of Abraham, and it is not limited in how many seeds he has. As part of the seed of Abraham all the saved have an inheritance in heaven we will all take part in that inheritance.

CHAPTER FOUR

Galatians 4:1-31
Now I say, That the heir, as long as he is a child, differeth nothing from a servant, though he be lord of all; But is under tutors and governors until the time appointed of the father. Even so we, when we were children, were in bondage under the elements of the world: But when the fulness of the time was come, God sent forth his Son, made of a woman, made under the law, To redeem them that were under the law, that we might receive the adoption of sons. And because ye are sons, God hath sent forth the Spirit of his Son into your hearts, crying, Abba, Father. Wherefore thou art no more a

servant, but a son; and if a son, then an heir of God through Christ. Howbeit then, when ye knew not God, ye did service unto them which by nature are no gods. But now, after that ye have known God, or rather are known of God, how turn ye again to the weak and beggarly elements, whereunto ye desire again to be in bondage? Ye observe days, and months, and times, and years. I am afraid of you, lest I have bestowed upon you labour in vain. Brethren, I beseech you, be as I am; for I am as ye are: ye have not injured me at all. Ye know how through infirmity of the flesh I preached the gospel unto you at the first. And my temptation which was in my flesh ye despised not, nor rejected; but received me as an angel of God, even as Christ Jesus. Where is then the blessedness ye spake of? for I bear you record, that, if it had been possible, ye would have plucked out your own eyes, and have given them to me. Am I therefore become your enemy, because I tell you the truth? They zealously affect you, but not well; yea, they would exclude you, that ye might affect them. But it is good to be zealously affected always in a good thing, and not only when I am present with you. My little children, of whom I travail in birth again until Christ be formed in you, I desire to be present with you now, and to change my voice; for I stand in doubt of you. Tell me, ye that desire to be under the law, do ye not hear the law? For it is written, that Abraham had two sons, the one by a bondmaid, the other by a freewoman. But he who was of the bondwoman was born after the flesh; but he of the freewoman was by promise. Which things are an allegory: for these are the two covenants; the one from the mount Sinai, which gendereth to bondage, which is Agar. For this Agar is mount Sinai in Arabia, and answereth to Jerusalem which now is, and is in bondage with her children. But Jerusalem which is above is free, which is the mother of us all. For it is written, Rejoice, thou barren that bearest not; break forth and cry, thou that travailest not: for the desolate hath many more children than she which hath an husband. Now we, brethren, as Isaac was, are the children of promise. But as then he that was born after the flesh persecuted him that was born after the Spirit, even so it is now. Nevertheless what saith the scripture? Cast out the bondwoman and her son: for the son of the bondwoman shall not be heir with the son of the freewoman. So then, brethren,

we are not children of the bondwoman, but of the free.

COMMENTARY

4:1 Now I say, That the heir, as long as he is a child, differeth nothing from a servant, though he be lord of all; The Gift of salvation that allows a person to be saved as was said in the last verse of the last chapter, is that we that are saved are now heirs of the Lord, we have an inheritance in heaven, it does not matter if we are a servant, or a lord (boss), a janitor, a preacher, whatever, the inheritance is the same (for all that are saved) in heaven no matter what your status here is on earth.

4:2 But is under tutors and governors until the time appointed of the father. The heir in the last verse is the saved person, if that saved person is a servant on earth his position on earth does not change just because he is saved, he remains a servant until such time as he is released or set free.

We as Christians are under the authority of our government, and laws of our countries, good, bad, or otherwise, we are held in bondage by the things of this world. The only acceptable time to rebel against the government is when that government tells us to do things that go against the word of God then we are to obey God and not man.

4:3 Even so we, when we were children, were in bondage under the elements of the world: we as people are under the law, we are to obey the law, as the law was established to judge sin and sinful behavior. As children born in this world we are under these elements. In simpler terms without Jesus Christ all we have is the law to be our guide, the law cannot now nor ever can save us, all it can do is judge us and let us continue on the path to the lake of fire for all eternity, that is the bondage of the law.

4:4 But when the fulness of the time was come, God sent forth his Son, made of a woman, made under the law, When the right time came, and in God's timing he sent Jesus who lived in the world in a human body, he was under that bondage of that human body just as we are. Jesus felt everything that you and I have felt, he hurt, he was tired, he got frustrated, he was hungry, etc. he was living under the bondage that the human sinful nature brings, yet he was without sin.

God sent Jesus to be the Saviour of the world. He sent his only son to be that perfect sinless sacrifice for our sins, including mine and yours, Jesus made that payment for our sins so we can receive that free gift of salvation and be freed from the bondage of that sin nature which leads to the lake of fire. Jesus was born just as you and I are now through the birth canal of a woman, who was made pregnant by the Holy Spirit.

4:5 To redeem them that were under the law, that we might receive the adoption of sons. Jesus came so we could be saved. This verse is clear that salvation is not an automatic action placed on a person just because they are saved, it is a gift that must be received by that person.

I look at salvation this way, take for instance, I have a million dollars on credit that I prepaid at an ice cream shop, and I stand outside with a sign that says free ice cream. All that person has to do is to go in and order what they want and then they say please apply some of that credit to my bill and then my bill is paid in full.

I can go in and place that million dollars on credit at that store, however if no one goes in and gets that free ice cream, it just sits there, and if everyone comes in for the free ice cream then the payment for that ice cream has already been made. This is the same that Jesus did for us on that cross, he made the payment for our sins, all we have to do is ask for it to be applied to our debt that we owe, then it is paid in full, praise the Lord.

4:6 And because ye are sons, God hath sent forth the Spirit of his Son into your hearts, crying, Abba, Father. Once we are saved we are given the Holy Spirt that, He lives, and dwells in us. The Holy Spirit is sealed in us until we reach eternity, or if it is easier to understand the Holy Spirit lives and is sealed in us until we take our last breath (Ephesians 4:30).

The Holy Spirit cries, he moans for us, he wants us to walk the way of the Lord, and when we don't it hurts his heart for us. The Holy Spirit cries Abba, Father. Abba simply defined is: *Father*, it is used in an intimate way to describe the father, almost like the supreme father. Fathers are loving, judging, strong, caring, etc., but when used as Abba Father it refers to the loving nature of the father, the father side of the father if that makes sense, it is the highest honor a father can be called by any person. We see here that the Holy Spirit calls God by the highest honor he can, Abba Father.

4:7 Wherefore thou art no more a servant, but a son; and if a son, then an heir of God

through Christ. Because of the holy Spirit living in us that are saved, and because we are saved, we are no longer under an eternal bondage. We may still be in bondage here on this earth but now we are saved, and now our eternal home is in heaven. Those that do not get saved, they are in bondage to their sin and if they die without Jesus as their Saviour, that bondage of that sin will keep them on that path until they reach the lake of fire.

4:8 Howbeit then, when ye knew not God, ye did service unto them which by nature are no gods. When you were lost, without Jesus as your Savior you served the idol gods, these idols are made by man to be worshiped by man. It has always amazed me how a person can make out of wood, metal, or stone an image and then worship and serve that image that they made expecting that image they made to save them. It is only God himself that can save a lost soul, and without being saved one lives and serves the Devil.

4:9 But now, after that ye have known God, or rather are known of God, how turn ye again to the weak and beggarly elements, whereunto ye desire again to be in bondage? The question is being asked here, how can you even think about going back to these false dead idols and begin to worship them again. You did that when you were dead in your sins and now you are not only known by God, but you are a child of God and run right back to the things you left which God himself hates.

These false idols and things that you do put you in bondage to sin. Sin always puts people in bondage, it always takes captive and before you know it, you have lost everything you ever had and sometimes even the people that were once put in your life for your help.

4:10 Ye observe days, and months, and times, and years. Paul is telling these saints here at this church that they focus on manmade holidays, they have a focus on times, seasons, years, but it seems they did not have that kind of a focus on the things of God.

4:11 I am afraid of you, lest I have bestowed upon you labour in vain. Paul says he is afraid of this church and what they have becomes and the idols and sin that they have let in since his last time with them. He is concerned if he has laboured with them in vain. He says I'm afraid I may have wasted my time with you. Is what he is thinking.

4:12 Brethren, I beseech you, be as I am; for I am as ye are: ye have not injured me at all. Paul is pleading with these folks to be like he is. Paul is separated from the things of the world, he does not go to the night clubs, the bars, hang out with ungodly people. Paul also tells them that he is just like they are, he is a Christian who is a child of God and that he has faced all these same temptations.

One thing about living for the Lord is that Satan will try everything in his power to get the bible believer to sin, he offers huge temptations that many Christians fall into. I fell into temptation at one time in my life, and you can read about my testimony in my book,[4] I went down a path that cost me everything, and it took a while to come back from my sins and the hurt that was caused by them. This is what falling into that sinful temptation will cost you.

Paul also tells this church that they have not harmed him by their choice to allow these false teachers into their church, Paul is broken hearted, as any one of us should be but he is not injured, they have injured themselves spiritually

---

[4] See the Authors work "Redemption: A True-Life Prodigal"

and may cost them physically for following after these false doctrines.

4:13 Ye know how through infirmity of the flesh I preached the gospel unto you at the first. Paul says you know that in prison, in beatings, in pain and anguish, I preached the gospel to you. You have been made aware that this was not an easy task to bring the message of the cross to this hate filled world, but there are some that are longing for the gospel message.

Folks this is still true today, yes the world seems to be at its height of evilness, but there are people in this world that still need Jesus and we must do our best to reach them with the gospel of Jesus Christ.

4:14 And my temptation which was in my flesh ye despised not, nor rejected; but received me as an angel of God, even as Christ Jesus. Paul says that even when they knew about how he had killed the Christians before he met Jesus and they knew how he persecuted them many times over that they still received him.

They did not despise him, but they received him as a brother in Christ, as an angel of God and they even received him as easily as they received the Lord Jesus Christ. We are to receive those into our house and churches that want to serve and love the Lord, we are to receive those that want to get saved into the church as well, we just must be guarded with the lost when they come in, so they do not spread the falseness of sin to the people in the church.

4:15 Where is then the blessedness ye spake of? for I bear you record, that, if it had been possible, ye would have plucked out your own eyes, and have given them to me. Paul is asking the saint in this church here where is this love that you had, what happened to the blessings you had received from the Lord, there was a time that you would have put out your own eyes and given them to me if I needed them, what happened to that kind of love that you had.

This is the kind of love that when you draw closer to God is made manifest in you, it is the kind of love that shows Jesus in you the hope of Glory, as a person draws closer to God the fruits of the spirt start to become who they are, loving others is automatically done, giving is automatically done, receiving those in the faith is automatically done this is that life changing stuff that walking the way of the Lord brings, and the blessings that come as a result of it is amazing.

4:16 Am I therefore become your enemy, because I tell you the truth? Paul is asking a question more as a statement than anything else, Paul is basically asking them that since they have followed these false teachers and they have fell into the sins of the world do they now hate him because he tells them the truth? I'm sure they fell like they do.

Look at Jesus, the Jews, his own people, hated him because they were loving living in their sin, and he told them the truth and they hated the truth. Advance to our time two thousand years to the year twenty twenty-two and you know what? People hate Jesus and us as Christians because we bible believing Christians have to tell people the truth and they hate that truth.

Truth requires accountability, it makes one examine his own self and then requires that person to remove the sin that is their lives, but they love their sin so much that they will persecute the messenger because they hate the message.

Want to test this, go to the local street corner, and hold up a sign that says, “homosexuality is a sin” or “fornication is a sin” and watch how many people get mad at you, on the sing that says Fornication is a sin, you will have many Christians getting mad at you as well.

The bible tells us that the truth will set you free (John 8:32) because the truth should convict that sinful heart to repent and turn back to God and the things of God, however again people love their sin, and their sinful lifestyle, so they instead of making the change in their lives, they reject the truth. Take for an example, a person speeds while driving and runs a stop sign, the police officer pulls him over and gives him the ticket, he argues with the officer but still ends up with a heavy costing ticket, that person, the majority of the time will not see that he was the one that was wrong and needs to not speed, but instead he will hate the police officer because he was the one that stopped him and gave him the ticket.

4:17 They zealously affect you, but not well; yea, they would exclude you, that ye might affect them. Zealously simply defined is: *filled with zeal*. The false teacher had a lot of zeal and did a good job compelling the believers to reject the truth of the God's word and follow after them.

If the false teachers had not influenced these believers to follow after their doctrines they would have then rejected them because the believer would have had to tell them the truth and they would have hated that truth. The false teacher would have had to exclude the believers and get away from them because they would not have like the message they were preaching and teaching.

4:18 But it is good to be zealously affected always in a good thing, and not only when I am present with you. Paul says it is a very good thing to be affected and to have that zeal but only for the good things, and that it is even better to have that zeal when he is not with them.

This is what we call today being on fire for the Lord. The Christians here in this church seem to be followers and not leaders. When Paul was with them they followed after his teachings, when someone else came along they followed after him, this happens when people are not seeking the Lord, this is also why it is crucial that the man of God that is put in the church as the

Pastor, is a God-called man as he will lead people to the Lord and not away from the Lord.

4:19 My little children, of whom I travail in birth again until Christ be formed in you, Travail simply defined is: *a painful, or laborious nature*. Paul is saying here that he will have to labor for these saints again as if they are children and brand new to the faith until they get stronger in their faith. Until Christ is formed in them simply means until they are grounded on the truth of the word of God, and they have enough convictions to stand up against anything that comes in and tries to destroy, basically Paul is saying here that he will start all over again in his prayers, and fasting for them.

4:20 I desire to be present with you now, and to change my voice; for I stand in doubt of you. Paul wishes that he could be with them and not be so upset with them. He says he wants to change his voice; he means that he is frustrated with these saints and wants not to be, he feels that if he were with them that he would be able to influence them differently and back to the things of the Lord.

Oh how we as Christians need to speak up about things for the Lord. Sin is sin plain and simple and sin must be rejected and removed, so the Holy Spirt can rule and reign in us and get us back to the things of the Lord.

4:21 Tell me, ye that desire to be under the law, do ye not hear the law? Paul is asking the ones that want to be under the law, the ones that went back to their sins, do they not listen to the law (sin) and how it binds people?

Notice here also my dear reader friend, that he uses the phrase “ye that desire” this shows that it was not all the saints in this church that were like this, it was not all of them that went back to Egypt so to speak.

4:22 For it is written, that Abraham had two sons, the one by a bondmaid, the other by a freewoman. The two sons of Abraham, who the blessed blood line was through, he had two sons, he had one through a bondwoman because they were trying to help God and the other he had with his wife, the bond woman was basically a slave, and the wife was the free woman.

4:23 But he who was of the bondwoman was born after the flesh; but he of the freewoman was by promise. Yes both were born from human women, but this means that the one son who was born in the flesh was not the son that God blessed or had planned to give them for the promise of his seed to remain forever. It was not the plan that God had.

That son was born because Sarah, Abrahams wife did not want to wait on God to provide them a son so she gave her bondwoman to Abraham so he could have a child with her, then she would take that son and make it her own, however then God allowed for Sarah to have a child called Isaac whom was the one God had planned for them to have anyway, he was the one of the promise.

4:24 Which things are an allegory: for these are the two covenants; the one from the mount Sinai, which gendereth to bondage, which is Agar. These two children are sort of an example (an allegory) of the bondage of sin by the one son who was born in the flesh, and the freedom that comes for the Lord by the son of promise.

4:25 For this Agar is mount Sinai in Arabia, and answereth to Jerusalem which now is, and is in bondage with her children. Notice that Jerusalem is the one that represents the free in Christ and that freedom in the Lord overcomes the bondage of sin, as the city that is in the sin nature must answer to the city of the Lord.

This is the allegory, the example of what freedom in the Lord is like and how the rejection of the Lord leads to bondage, an if one remains in the bondage, they will step into eternity being in torments. Luke 16:19-31

4:26 But Jerusalem which is above is free, which is the mother of us all. Jerusalem is the city of the Lord it is the city that represents the Lord and the freedom in Christ, in the book of Revelation we see that we the saved will live in the city the new Jerusalem. This is the city that that is huge the bible describes just how big it actually is.

4:27 For it is written, Rejoice, thou barren that bearest not; break forth and cry, thou that travailest not: for the desolate hath many more children than she which hath an husband. Simply put, there are many more of the lost world than there ever will be of the believers. The bible tells us in Matthew 7:12-14 that it is very few people that will come to faith in the Lord compared to the many that will follow after the ways of sin. The desolate, the lost, those that live in sin will have by nature more children than the married ones will.

This was that two covenants mentioned in verse twenty-four Abrahams seed was promised to be multiplied, so the one son conceived outside of God's plan was multiplied in the ways of the world and the other son, whom God did bless his seed was also multiplied but not as much as the that of the world.

4:28 Now we, brethren, as Isaac was, are the children of promise. We are of the seed of Isaac, the children of promise and all who are or get saved become part of that seed, that blood line.

4:29 But as then he that was born after the flesh persecuted him that was born after the Spirit, even so it is now. The seed of the son that was born out of the will of the Lord hated the blessed son because he was rejected by his father, and that hatred has continued until today, the world hates the true Christians and wants nothing to do with them, if the world cannot change their beliefs they will try to kill them. (II Timothy 3:12)

4:30 Nevertheless what saith the scripture? Cast out the bondwoman and her son: for the son of the bondwoman shall not be heir with the son of the freewoman. The bible said to cast out the bondwoman, her son that was born because of a sinful choice, and was not to associate with God's choice.

This my dear reader friend is crucial, and you see this discussed all through the bible as we are to separate ourselves form those that are living in sin and not following the Lord. I can tell you for sure, those that do not love the Lord will never help you to serve the Lord.

4:31 So then, brethren, we are not children of the bondwoman, but of the free. Paul again reminds the saints here that we as believers are not of the bondwoman, we are no longer of the seed of the son born in sin, but we are now of the seed of the free son, the one that God blessed the blood line through.

CHAPTER FIVE

Galatians 5:1-26

Stand fast therefore in the liberty wherewith Christ hath made us free, and be not entangled again with the yoke of bondage. Behold, I Paul say unto you, that if ye be circumcised, Christ shall profit you nothing. For I testify again to every man that is circumcised, that he is a debtor to do the whole law. Christ is become of no effect unto you, whosoever of you are justified by the law; ye are fallen from grace. For we through the Spirit wait for the hope of righteousness by faith. For in Jesus Christ neither circumcision availeth any thing, nor uncircumcision; but faith which worketh by love. Ye did run well; who did hinder you that ye should not obey the truth? This persuasion cometh not of him that calleth you. A little leaven leaveneth the whole lump. I have confidence in you through the Lord, that ye will be none otherwise minded: but he

that troubleth you shall bear his judgment, whosoever he be. And I, brethren, if I yet preach circumcision, why do I yet suffer persecution? then is the offence of the cross ceased. I would they were even cut off which trouble you. For, brethren, ye have been called unto liberty; only use not liberty for an occasion to the flesh, but by love serve one another. For all the law is fulfilled in one word, even in this; Thou shalt love thy neighbour as thyself. But if ye bite and devour one another, take heed that ye be not consumed one of another. This I say then, Walk in the Spirit, and ye shall not fulfil the lust of the flesh. For the flesh lusteth against the Spirit, and the Spirit against the flesh: and these are contrary the one to the other: so that ye cannot do the things that ye would. But if ye be led of the Spirit, ye are not under the law. Now the works of the flesh are manifest, which are these; Adultery, fornication, uncleanness, lasciviousness, Idolatry, witchcraft, hatred, variance, emulations, wrath, strife, seditions, heresies, Envyings, murders, drunkenness, revellings, and such like: of the which I tell you before, as I have also told you in time past, that they which do such things shall not inherit the kingdom of God. But the fruit of the Spirit is

love, joy, peace, longsuffering, gentleness, goodness, faith, Meekness, temperance: against such there is no law. And they that are Christ's have crucified the flesh with the affections and lusts. If we live in the Spirit, let us also walk in the Spirit. Let us not be desirous of vain glory, provoking one another, envying one another.

COMMENTARY

5:1 Stand fast therefore in the liberty wherewith Christ hath made us free, and be not entangled again with the yoke of bondage. Paul is telling this church to stay faithful in the liberty, the freedom, that was given to them by Christ and his sacrifice on the cross. Liberty is a word that many Christians use a lot and most of them misuse this word to live anyway they want as they say, well I am saved and going to heaven so I can do what I want. To a point that is true, they are saved, and they can choose to live how they want, however the bible also tells us that they will have to answer for those choices, that if they choose to live like the world they will reap benefits of the world and will still have to answer to God for their choices.

Paul is telling these Saints here not to get entangled back into the bondage of sin as to which they were set free from. He is NOT telling them that they will lose or can lose their salvation, he is telling them that they can get in a carnal state of mind and be at odds with God and that they will reap the judgement of God on them as the bible tells us that God chastens those whom he loves. (Hebrews 12:6)

5:2 Behold, I Paul say unto you, that if ye be circumcised, Christ shall profit you nothing. Paul is telling the saints here that if they are still under the law, which when a person was a believer they would have to show that by being circumcised, then Christ is of no affect to them. If they are under the law they cannot be saved as Christ is who brings salvation, and not the things of the world, not the law. If it is the law that saves them then Christ shall be of no profit, no gain for them.

5:3 For I testify again to every man that is circumcised, that he is a debtor to do the whole law. If you live by the law and rely on that for your salvation then you are obligated to obey every bit of that law, every jot and every tittle you are required to obey, that if you mess up on just one part of it, or break one part of it in any way you are guilty of all. I praise the Lord that salvation allows for us to still be saved even though we at times mess up.

5:4 Christ is become of no effect unto you, whosoever of you are justified by the law; ye are fallen from grace. If they believe that it is the law that saves them, then Christ and his death on the cross was useless and of no affect on them, Paul tells them then that they are fallen from grace. If they can be saved by the law then they have lost their salvation.

All false religions will require some kind of works salvation. All of these religions and beliefs all deny that Jesus Christ is the only way to heaven, and if they have a works salvation they can live and do what they want, they can change and corrupt the bible how they choose to fit their belief system and justify their sin and still the moment they step into eternity they will lift their eyes in torments in hell.

5:5 For we through the Spirit wait for the hope of righteousness by faith. Salvation is and has always been by faith in Jesus Christ. The difficulty that the natural man cannot understand is that they only believe in what they can see. If you only believe in what you see then it is not faith, faith in knowing deep down inside of you that something will work out and going for that until you reach that goal.

For us that are saved we believe with every ounce of our being that Christ died on the cross for our sins, was buried and rose again that third day. Our faith is that Jesus saved us and once we believe that, and called upon him, our faith is made real. When the Lord answers our prayers, it is made real when we take what the bible says and apply it to our lives, our faith is made real when we step into eternity, and we meet Jesus face to face. As a saved person we wait for our hope to be made real, that is the hope of righteousness, that hope of perfection it is all by faith, and faith alone.

5:6 For in Jesus Christ neither circumcision availeth any thing, nor uncircumcision; but faith which worketh by love. In Christ it does not matter if you were circumcised under the law or not circumcised under the law, we are saved by grace and ALL, anyone, everyone, rich, poor, whomever can receive that salvation as long as they believe and as a result of that belief they call on the name of the Lord.

I often say when a person loves the Lord, I mean falling in love with him, they are in the word, they are seeking God with all their heart, mind, and soul then they will begin to reflect the fruits of the spirit which we will see in verse twenty-two. These fruits of the Spirit produce love, they produce the things of God reflecting through your life, this is your faith being shown in love by Jesus Christ our Lord.

5:7 Ye did run well; who did hinder you that ye should not obey the truth? Paul is telling them that they were walking by faith and reflecting the fruits of the Spirt in their lives and in their church, however they had gotten away from that. Paul is inquiring about who had gotten them, off track, who had diverted them from continuing in that walk.

If a person is not in the word of God every day and not seeking God on a daily basis they will be led astray. A person does not have to be an evil person to fall into sin or to backslide, all they have to do is stop putting the things of God in their lives and they by their sin nature will drift toward the world.

5:8 This persuasion cometh not of him that calleth you. The one that persuaded these saints to divert from their faith, and caused them to get to that backslidden state were people that were not of the Lord. It was the Lord that was calling them to walk in him, but the world called them to walk in the ways of the world.

The world will cause you to doubt your salvation, they will cause you to question your faith, they will cause you to not trust in the bible, it is not the Lord that causes this, it is those that are not seeking the Lord that causes you to do that.

I learnt a principle a long time ago, that simply says "those that do not love the Lord, will NOT help you to serve the Lord" this is a true principle and should be remembered when it comes to all people in your life, choose wisely. I use this principle for all people I allow in my life or not allow in my life.

5:9 A little leaven leaveneth the whole lump. It takes just one person not believing, or not seeking the Lord to get you to stop serving and seeking the Lord. Ever been in a church where people are fighting, or have contention with one another, I have, I participated in it at times, well those, including myself, that were of that contentious mindset, would hinder those that were serving the Lord form doing their job, I would be hindered at times myself. This was discouraging to me and to others and that discouragement led to others and myself quitting what we were doing for the Lord as a result and not seeking him any longer. As a result I now am extremely selective who I allow in my close circle of friends and mentors in my life.

5:10 I have confidence in you through the Lord, that ye will be none otherwise minded: but he that troubleth you shall bear his judgment, whosoever he be. Paul seems to be shifting from a form of rebuke to exhortation, he is offering confidence to these saints. Paul has expressed his frustrations with them, pointed out the errors of their ways, and is now trying to get them back on track.

He tells them that he is confident that they will remain in their walk with God, that they will grow in their faith and learn to not weaver, and that they will not follow anything that does not line up with scripture.

Paul also tells these saints that that person or persons that led them astray will have to answer to God for that as well. The bible does tell us that we will all stand before the God of the bible one day and answer for what we have done or who we have led away from him, and these folks that led this church away from the things of God will be judged by God accordingly.

5:11 And I, brethren, if I yet preach circumcision, why do I yet suffer persecution? then is the offence of the cross ceased. Paul is proving again that he is preaching and teaching the truth. He is saying here that if he preaches what they want to hear, that it is circumcision that saves, then they would love that and not persecute him, they would not be mad at him, it is the truth that makes people mad, it is the truth that hurts people feelings because it is the truth that corrects a person and gets them to the Lord. I often say that truth requires accountability, it is this accountability that makes people mad.

Try as an example, walk up to someone that is vain in themselves, their appearance is off a little and maybe even a little heavy, you go to that person and tell them that they are fat and oh man you had better run as they will want to kill you, did you lie to them? no, but they did not want to hear that truth and that truth made them mad at you.

This is the same with the gospel message, people think it is them that gets them to heaven, some spend their entire lives getting themselves to heaven to which they end up in hell, just to find out the bible was true after all, and it is only through Jesus Christ that they get to heaven. Oh how the truth is hated.

5:12 I would they were even cut off which trouble you. Simply put, Paul is saying that he wishes that these people were not even around the saints so they could not be led astray any longer. Folks it is crucial that we only allow those seeking the same God of the bible that we are, in our lives, so we do not get led astray. It takes one small compromise with someone that is not seeking God, that will lead to many more compromises with you and soon, very soon, you will be walking in the things of the world.

5:13 For, brethren, ye have been called unto liberty; only use not liberty for an occasion to the flesh, but by love serve one another. Paul is stating here that as Christians that they have a certain liberty, a certain freedom to do things. They are saved and can never be unsaved, they cannot lose their salvation(Ephesians 4:30) so in a sense they can sort of do what they want and still go to heaven.

This is a doctrine that has plagued Christianity since the cross of Jesus. Many Christians feel that they can live how they want, they can smoke, drink, fornicate and since they are saved that they have that liberty to do so.

Unlike the smoking and drinking, fornication is a sin listed in the bible, the other two are not, however the bible does tell us about weights that can hinder a person from coming to Christ and one Christians smoking, drinking, cussing, etc. can be a stumbling block.

The bible does tell us that yes, we have that liberty to do things, not all things are good to do, and just because we can does not mean we should. We can go into a bar, sit at the counter order food and a soda we have that liberty to do so, but there is always that possibility that someone was driving by and saw you walk into that bar, now that has become a stumbling block for that person as now they say that you are no better than them.

The liberty that we have in the Lord was not intended for us not to serve the Lord as there will be consequences for that (Romans 8:1), but it is intended for us to serve the Lord with all our hearts, minds, and souls. This was the intent; we have that freedom to serve the Lord out of love and not out of being forced to do so.

5:14 For all the law is fulfilled in one word, even in this; Thou shalt love thy neighbour as thyself. Everything that the law tried to accomplish was that we love one another. We are to love our neighbor as ourselves. In the Old testament we have many chapters on the law, on keeping the law, and the punishments for not keeping the law, however in the New Testament, we have just two basic commandments, the first of which is to love the Lord thy God with all thy heart, mind , and soul, the second is almost the same but we are to love our neighbor as ourselves. (Matthew 22:37-39)

5:15 But if ye bite and devour one another, take heed that ye be not consumed one of another. This verse is basically saying that if you treat others badly do not be surprised when they treat you badly either. If you are always sowing contention and discord among others you will receive the same kind of treatment from others. If you choose to sow the things of God to others, and to show them love no matter who they are, you will receive the love and blessings not necessarily from man or even the person that you mistreat, but you will receive that love and blessings for the Lord himself as it is something that he has commanded you to do. Receiving his love is the best love to receive.

5:16 This I say then, Walk in the Spirit, and ye shall not fulfil the lust of the flesh. I live by this verse; it serves as a great reminder of the sin that I was once dwelling and living in. To walk in the Spirit one must be intentional in their pursuit of the Lord.

The bible tells us over and over again that we are to seek, to search, to draw nigh, we are to take that step, it is not always easy to do so, but once we make that commitment to seek for him we will find him. If we are constantly putting the things of God in our lives, by reading and studying our bibles, by being in prayer, we will be walking in the Spirt and will not fulfill that lust of the flesh.

Please do not be misled, you will still have those fleshly temptations, you will still be enticed by the thought of sin, but walking in the Spirit reminds you of scripture, it reminds you of the Lord, and it reminds you of where you once were and that you do not want to go back down that path ever again. I still fight the temptations of my old sin filled life that I was living in for many years, but I have put on the whole armour of God and by the help of the Holy Spirit, I am able to recognize and reject that temptation. It took many years to do so.

5:17 For the flesh lusteth against the Spirit, and the Spirit against the flesh: and these are contrary the one to the other: so that ye cannot do the things that ye would. Your sinful fleshly body will always want to drag you to sin. Ever notice that you leave church on Sunday morning having been filled with the Holy Spirt and all is good, then that afternoon you are thinking about the things at church that morning while installing a towel rack in the house for your wife, then out of nowhere you go to tap in that plastic anchor and you break a hole in the wall, your first reaction is usually to cuss, usually to say a few choice words at that moment, that my friend is our sin nature.

With the Holy Spirit living in us we now have the victory to overcome that, yes we may still say a word or two when we are on our own, or we find ourselves getting frustrated over stupid selfish stuff and we want to lash out, however we do not because we have the Holy Spirit in us. I cannot speak for you, but for me I sometimes cuss out loud to the Lord instead of out loud to a person, God allows for me to vent to him, to clear the frustrations out of my heart, so then he can work through me. Our flesh and the Holy Spirit living in us are constantly at war with one another, which ever one you feed is the one that wins.

5:18 But if ye be led of the Spirit, ye are not under the law. If we are saved we are not under the law. If we live the way of the Lord we will have that freedom in the Lord to serve and to love others as he had designed us to do. We are no longer bound to the law or the consequences of the law because God has saved us through Jesus Christ.

Please do NOT misunderstand me, when we use the term law we are not referring to the society laws that we have today, in other words if the speed limit is fifty-five then anything over that you will still get a ticket and have fines to pay. This law is talking about the spiritual law, the law that was in the Old Testament, the laws today are not for salvation or our walk with God, we have the bible for that, our laws are for a peaceable society to live and dwell in peace with one another.

5:19 Now the works of the flesh are manifest, which are these; Adultery, fornication, uncleanness, lasciviousness, The next few verses will describe the works of the flesh and the fruits of the Spirit. The biggest thing to remember in these verses is that whatever lifestyle you are currently living you will reflect one of these fruits, the fruits of the flesh or the fruits of the Spirit.

The bible tells us in Matthew 7:20 that you shall know a person by their fruits. Take for example, a person that comes into a church and begins to talk about, we need to do this, or we need to do that, we can change this or we can change that, they will usually put up a godly front but as the bible says they will have a form of godliness but they will deny that power thereof.

This type of a person you need to let them come and just watch them for a while, see what their fruits are, do their fruits match up to their speech? You can hide a lot of things from people but your true fruits of who you are will come out at some point. If you are walking in the spirit the things of God will become who you are without even trying, if you are not walking in the Spirit then the things of the flesh become who you are.

These are some of the works (fruits) of the flesh: **the following verses are split, and words are capitalized for emphasis only and not to reflect any change in the text or punctuation of the Holy Bible King James Version, all words in bold print are the words used in the bible**

Adultery biblically defined is: *being separated from your wife and living with another woman as your wife without divorcing the first wife*[5].

Fornication biblically defined is: *having sex with anyone to whom you are not married to.*

Uncleanness simply defined is: *morally or spiritually impure, one whose heart is focused on the sins of this world.*

Lasciviousness simply defined is: *lustful sexual desire.* Oh man how this one is one that so many men in the faith get caught up in, I know this from past experience.

[5] See the authors work "the Biblical Family: from Beginning to Blended" for a complete study on biblical adultery

5:20 Idolatry simply defined is: *worshiping physical objects as God*. This makes a mockery of almighty God.

Witchcraft biblically defined is: *Satan worship*. The bible also tells us that rebellion, even rebellion to the call of God on one's life is considered like the sin of witchcraft (I Samuel 15:23).

Hatred simply defined is: *extreme dislike or hate toward a person.* One of the first signs that a person is living in the works of the flesh is that they will start to let you know who they don't like and who they are angry with.

Variance simply defined is: *to be at odds with people*. In other words they will always have disagreements with other or always have a better way of doing things to the point of thinking the other one is dumb; it will not be just one person they are like this with it will be many.

Emulations simply defined is*: having to be better than the next person.* This is the person that always believes they are better then another and will always try to do things better than the other person or try to imitate someone great. For example when a young bible student graduates from bible college some of them think they can be just as effective and great as they think their pastor is, that they can be the next Billy Graham, they may even try to do crusades, but they will almost always fail as God has called them to be them and not the people they are trying to imitate.

Wrath simply defined is: *exercising that hate toward another person.* God will have wrath on those that hate him, but not until after they have had many chances to repent and turn from their sins, God's wrath is a wrath against sin and not people, however if people are insistent on worshiping that sin they will receive that wrath.

Strife simply defined is: *bitterness and contention.* Oh man how this has taken over the things and the people of God.

Seditions Simply defined is: *incitement of resistance or uprising against authority.* As Christians we are to stand for the things of the bible, but we are not to be the one that causes others to resist as well, we are not to cause people to upraise against their governments, their bosses or whatever, we are to make the choice for ourselves and just hold to biblical principles.

Heresies simply defined is: *the belief and teachings of false doctrines and religions.* In other words anything that does not line up with the bible is a heresy. Many people have many different heresies today and will try to teach them in the churches.

5:21 Envyings simply defined is: *resentful of things that other may have that you don't*. This is something that even as pastors we must carefully watch it is easy for us to be envious of another Pastors ministry and the success of that ministry when the ministry the Lord has given you is a small one.

Murders simply defined is*: intentionally killing someone out of anger or envy*. You can be so envious of another person and what they have that you want to kill them, you can have greed toward another man, or want his wife, or whatever. All the previous sins listed in this passage can all lead to murder if that sinful fleshly desire is not placed under control, you gain that control from the Holy Spirit living in you.

Drunkenness simply defined is: *excessive use of alcohol*. Alcohol has destroyed many people and many marriages and many in the Christian realm are struggling with this as well. Many will try to hide it, but they usually always fail. I have seen firsthand in the ministry how this drunkenness has destroyed some men and their service for the Lord himself.

Revellings simply defined is: *intense pleasure*. This is the kind of pleasure that leads to rape, murder, a rejection of all moral restraints, drugs, etc.

and such like: of the which I tell you before, as I have also told you in time past, that they which do such things shall not inherit the kingdom of God. These people that live in these sins are not Christian and are lost and on their way to hell. Let me be clear here, a Christian can live in this sin, but he will face conviction and chastisement from the Lord, he will know he is not supposed to do these things.

A lost person will only know these things and for them it is normal, and they do not have any conviction in them as the Holy Spirit is not living in them. It is possible for a Christian to have a hardened heart to the things of God, but they will not be able to deny the Holy Spirit living in them, they will not be able to deny that they are living in sin, and they will most definitely not want to be around any Christians or churches as it increases that conviction. It is the ones that deny anything of God that you have to watch out for.

5:22 But the fruit of the Spirit is love, joy, peace, longsuffering, gentleness, goodness, faith, the next things are the fruits of the Spirit. These are the fruits that will automatically come to a person who is seeking God, the more of the Lord one seeks, the more these fruits become who they are. I am a personal example of that transformation from the works of the flesh to the fruits of the Spirit.

Love biblically defined is: *dying to yourself for the sake of others.* This is the simplest explanation I can give for love. If we love our wives, children, parents, etc. we will give our lives for them. If we love others we will love them at the cost of our own lives. The apostles laid down their lives for others so they could come to Jesus (John 15:13)

Joy simply defined is: *to experience great pleasure.* This is not a worldly, sinful pleasure, but a godly pleasure. When a soul gets saved after many hours invested in that person in prayer and witnessing, it is a joyful experience. It is a joyful experience when a person fully surrenders to the things of the Lord that is great joy

Peace simply defined is: *calmness in your life*. This kind of peace is a drama free life, I used to live a drama filled life, then after many years I got out of that lifestyle and now I enjoy the things of God which bring peace to my life.

Longsuffering simply defined is: *patiently enduring, patience.* This is a hard thing for us as Christians to do but the Lord does it for us, he has delayed his judgement for sin because he is patiently enduring the lost to come to him (II Peter 3:9)

Gentleness simply defined is: *being gentle*. It is important that the Christian be gentle in all he does. Being gentle reflects the heart of God in that saved person, it is great that this becomes a fruit in our spirit.

Goodness simply defined is: *having a mind focused on things above and not on things of the earth* (Colossians 3:2).

Faith simply defined is: *belief or trust in God*, also biblically defined is: *reading and studying the word of God, the bible* (Romans 10:17)

5:23 Meekness simply defined is: *humbleness*. This is being in a humble mindset and realizing that without the Lord you are nothing.

Temperance simply defined is: *restraining your bad reactions so they can glorify God*. As Christians when we walk with God we can tell the fruit of someone by how they respond to situations or people, if they react badly it means they are still working on their temperance. **: against such there is no law.** The bible tells us that there is no law for these fruits, you cannot be good enough to display them in your life, you cannot follow any law to truly have these traits in your heart, you only receive these traits from walking with the Lord, they become who you are, this is that part of a new man in Christ Jesus.

5:24 And they that are Christ's have crucified the flesh with the affections and lusts. Those that are saved have quenched the woks of the flesh, they fight the temptations, but they receive the victory over those temptations, in other words they do not give into those temptations when they arise. They will arise, but praise God by walking in the spirit they no longer have control over you.

5:25 If we live in the Spirit, let us also walk in the Spirit. If we are saved, and tell others that we are saved, then we need to walk that way. No greater destruction has ever come to the body of Christ than for those that are saved to live like the world. Oh how that has destroyed so many people in their walk and love for the Lord.

5:26 Let us not be desirous of vain glory, provoking one another, envying one another. Simply defined is: *we are not to take pride in what we do for the Lord, or even take pride in the fruits of the Spirit* as the moment we have that vain glory we begin our journey back to the works of the flesh.

I have said many times and will say again, you do not have to be an evil person to serve the works of the flesh, all you have to do is stop putting the things of God into your life. If you keep you bible closed, you will automatically display the works of the flesh in your life.

CHAPTER SIX

Galatians 6:1-18

Brethren, if a man be overtaken in a fault, ye which are spiritual, restore such an one in the spirit of meekness; considering thyself, lest thou also be tempted. Bear ye one another's burdens, and so fulfil the law of Christ. For if a man think himself to be something, when he is nothing, he deceiveth himself. But let every man prove his own work, and then shall he have rejoicing in himself alone, and not in another. For every man shall bear his own burden. Let him that is taught in the word communicate unto him

that teacheth in all good things. Be not deceived; God is not mocked: for whatsoever a man soweth, that shall he also reap. For he that soweth to his flesh shall of the flesh reap corruption; but he that soweth to the Spirit shall of the Spirit reap life everlasting. And let us not be weary in well doing: for in due season we shall reap, if we faint not. As we have therefore opportunity, let us do good unto all men, especially unto them who are of the household of faith. Ye see how large a letter I have written unto you with mine own hand. As many as desire to make a fair shew in the flesh, they constrain you to be circumcised; only lest they should suffer persecution for the cross of Christ. For neither they themselves who are circumcised keep the law; but desire to have you circumcised, that they may glory in your flesh. But God forbid that I should glory, save in the cross of our Lord Jesus Christ, by whom the world is crucified unto me, and I unto the world. For in Christ Jesus neither circumcision availeth any thing, nor uncircumcision, but a new creature. And as many as walk according to this rule, peace be on them, and mercy, and upon the Israel of God. From henceforth let no man trouble me: for I bear in my body the marks of the

Lord Jesus. Brethren, the grace of our Lord Jesus Christ be with your spirit. Amen.

COMMENTARY

6:1 Brethren, if a man be overtaken in a fault, ye which are spiritual, restore such an one in the spirit of meekness; considering thyself, lest thou also be tempted. There are a couple of principles in this verse that we must highlight, the first of which is when we see a brother in Christ living a life not in line with the bible we should do our best to try and encourage them to get back to the Lord. This option will meet with a lot of resistance as almost all saved people living in a carnal state of mind will get mad and angry at you for telling them that what they are doing is wrong.

It is this type of a Christian that you must first for yourself be prayed up and have the prompting of the Holy Spirit to be able to do this. As it says, we are to let our brothers and sisters in Christ who are living in sin know that that is a bad path and they need to turn back to God, we must do this lovingly and not out of self-pride or arrogance.

Another principle is that we must make sure that we do not fall into the same sin, or even a sin ourselves of judging our brother or sister without judging ourselves first. This verse does not tell every Christian to let every other Christian know that they are living in sin, it tells the Christian that is diligently and intentionally seeking God, those that are "spiritual" to be the ones that do this, in my opinion this would include the ones that are living a spiritual life and have the fruit of a spiritual life as well.

We are to try and restore a brother or sister back to the things of God so God can use them for his glory, and they can live a life pleasing to the Lord, oh what a Saviour.

6:2 Bear ye one another's burdens, and so fulfil the law of Christ. As bible believing Christians, children of God we are to bear the burdens of others, if one of the brothers is hurting we go and comfort them, if one of them is sick we check on them, whatever it is we be there for them, and help them get through this.

We in today's carnal church world will just tell someone oh man I'm sorry this is happening I will pray for you and the moment we walk away from that person we forget all about praying for them, but we remember to tell others about them which most of the time leads to gossip.

It is important that when someone in the church, or your life, is hurting that we are truly there for them, that we bathe them in prayer, that we sit with them, we talk with them and most importantly we shut our mouths and listen to them as they talk.

Just a little secret to bearing one another's burdens, they do not really want to know what you or someone you know or went through, they do not really care at that moment what you did to get out of a situation, all they really want at that time is for someone to listen to them, for someone to sympathize with them, and to love them, so in my opinion, from experience in doing this, just keep your mouth shut and just listen, and only offer a solution if they ask, once they are over their current emotional state then you can begin to offer that guidance and then they may begin to listen.

6:3 For if a man think himself to be something, when he is nothing, he deceiveth himself. If a man is puffed up, arrogant, thinking they are the bomb diggity then they deceive themselves. It is these types of people that will always tell you about what they have done, how much money they have, and how good they are, and how close to God they are but the fruits of their life will not reflect the things of God.

This type of a person deceives themselves; they are lying to themselves, and the pride of life gets in the way, it controls them, and they get to loving this pride, just remember what happened to Lucifer, he was so proudful that he wanted to be like the most high, and he thought he could overthrow God well his fate is in the lake of fire for all eternity.

6:4 But let every man prove his own work, and then shall he have rejoicing in himself alone, and not in another. A man's joy comes from success, when a Christian man is successful in the things of the Lord, if they are seeking God and the fruits of the Spirit are showing forth, they are proving their own work and are happy in themselves, they are not arrogant. This kind of happiness is a joyous happiness, it is one that produces a humbleness within that makes that person happy in the Lord. So let that person prove his own work, so he can have the happiness in himself and not just see the happiness in others.

6:5 For every man shall bear his own burden. We all have to bear our own burdens, yes we also are to help others to bear their burdens, but we are to bear our own. It is during our burdens that we grow, it is during these times of difficulty that we learn to draw closer to God, it is during these times that we also experience the true love of God on a different level than before. We are to endure the burdens of this life and know that the Lord walks with us through our enduring of our burdens.

6:6 Let him that is taught in the word communicate unto him that teacheth in all

good things. The one that is taught from the word of God should communicate to the one that teaches from the word of God. We are to pray to God for our help, we are to call upon him for our relief, we are to ask God for his guidance, we need to talk to those that teach us from the word they may have advice from experience that can help us get through what we need to get through.

6:7 Be not deceived; God is not mocked: for whatsoever a man soweth, that shall he also reap. There are many things in this life that it seems like that sin has taken control of, and many times it seems like sin is winning. We see this especially in the anti-bible and anti-God groups in our world.

Take for example the alphabet group, LGBQWERT or whatever they call themselves these days, this group flaunts their sin in the face of God, they are tempting and daring him, when society says we need to accept this, and get on board with this gender changing junk, it seems as if they are winning.

These are the times that we must rely on this verse, that we need not be deceived as well, God will judge them, he knows what is happening, he knows what is coming and he knows the wickedness of man's heart.

I said the other day in Sunday School, we, you and I, may never see some evil people get punished, or exposed in this world, but they, like us, all have to stand before the God of the bible and have to give an account of themselves to the same Lord you and I have to, that day my dear friend is a sure thing. What they reap they will sow.

The saddest thing for me especially with the alphabet group is that this mindset is beginning to be accepted by the churches in America. We see churches debating and splitting over this, we see carnal at best Christians, those that have a form of godliness but deny that power thereof (II Timothy 3:5) all beginning to accept this worldly, sinful, God-rejecting mindset in their churches, and not only that, they are making a mockery of the pulpit and the shepherd that is supposed to be a God called position, by placing these blatantly sin promoting people in the pulpit. As hard as this is to see, we must fall back on this verse, that whatsoever a man sows that he SHALL reap, their day, like ours is on the horizon and is coming.

6:8 For he that soweth to his flesh shall of the flesh reap corruption; but he that soweth to the Spirit shall of the Spirit reap life everlasting. Simply put, if you put in your life and focus on, the things of God, read your bible, be in constant prayer in your life, go to church and get involved so iron can sharpen iron, make sure to only allow people in your life that are chasing God just like you, then you will produce the fruits of the Spirit and begin to walk in them, this will end up being a natural happening and you will not even have to think about it.

You do not have to be an evil or even bad person to walk in the ways of the flesh, by nature, we have a sin nature that will drift toward evil things, all we have to do to walk in the flesh, and to focus on the sin in this world and to live in that sin is to NOT put the things of God in your life. If you stop going to church, if you keep your bible closed, if you do not pray or hang out with godly people you will find yourself cussing at times, accepting sinful sexual jokes as ok, not caring if others go to hell, only caring about you and your family, you will find yourself caring more for your success in this earthly life while neglecting the treasures of the eternal life. Yes you may be saved, sealed, complete, but you are not growing or walking in the Spirit because you are not feeding that spirit.

The saved person, those that are born-again have two natures in them, the flesh, and the Spirit, it is whatever one they feed is the one that is dominate. Guaranteed if you do not feed the side of the Holy Spirit in your life, than you will feed that sinful flesh of yours.

6:9 And let us not be weary in well doing: for in due season we shall reap, if we faint not. This is an excellent message of encouragement for the saints here at this church who have been reproved and rebuked by the apostle Paul who is now exhorting them in the Lord, he is telling them to not be weary, to keep on the faith, to encourage one another, to walk in the way of the Lord, he understands they will get tired and discouraged at times, but that they need to keep on keeping on.

This same verse is for us as Christians today, we need to not get discouraged, we need to keep on inviting, keep on witnessing, keep on praying for others, in Gods timing we will see some of this come to light.
My dear reader friend please do not be discouraged, please do not quit, you are loved,

you are important to the work of the Lord, and God just wants his best on your life and so should you.

6:10 As we have therefore opportunity, let us do good unto all men, especially unto them who are of the household of faith. As people come and go in our lives we are to do good unto them, but especially to those that are saved and born again.

We are to show the love of Christ to everyone. When we as Christians help and do good toward each other it builds up the cause for Christ and makes it stronger. Lord knows with all the recent deaths of saints and the evil pushing in harder, we need as many people on the Lord's side as possible, I for one will stand by you, will stand with you, and will stand alone if need be.

6:11 Ye see how large a letter I have written unto you with mine own hand. Paul had trouble with his vision he was going blind, and he usually had someone write what he dictated for the letters in the bible.

Paul was so upset and had such a broken heart for this church that he wrote this long letter to them with his own hand, he struggled to write it, but he did as the Lord led through the Holy Spirit. Paul is the author of many books in the New Testament, yes they are his words, word for word, as given to him by the Holy Spirit, but sometimes he had someone else pen them for him.

6:12 As many as desire to make a fair shew in the flesh, they constrain you to be circumcised; only lest they should suffer persecution for the cross of Christ. Many people wanted to have the appearance of the Lord on them but were not willing to suffer the persecution for the Lord. In simpler terms they were hypocrites, they only had that form of godliness but denied that power thereof.

These are the folks that when they are forced to cling to their faith or to compromise to the flesh, they will compromise to the flesh. They want the SHOW (shew) for others to see but when the going gets tough they quit.

6:13 For neither they themselves who are circumcised keep the law; but desire to have you circumcised, that they may glory in your flesh. Here it says that even though they themselves are circumcised, they themselves are "Christians" they are not walking that way, they are not living up to that appearance, they expect you to do so and will judge you for not and call you a hypocrite themselves.

I know this to be true, I was one of them for many years of my life even as a saved person I was just like these people. Be cautious of those that call out sin to you, see how they live their lives, you will tell by their fruit if they are walking with God or not. Usually the ones that are quick and arrogant to call out your sin and the sin of others are ones just like these described in this verse.

However if a godly person, that is walking with God points out a sin in your life, take it out of love, repent, and get that sin out of your life as God sent that person to tell you about that sin.

6:14 But God forbid that I should glory, save in the cross of our Lord Jesus Christ, by whom the world is crucified unto me, and I unto the world. Paul is reminding the saints here that he is doing what he does for the Lord, that he never wants an ounce of praise or glory for the things of the Lord. He is crucified by the world for his message of salvation that is only through Jesus Christ. Paul separates himself from the sinful things and sinful people of the world, he tells them about Jesus but does not keep company with them.

6:15 For in Christ Jesus neither circumcision availeth any thing, nor uncircumcision, but a new creature. In Christ, or simpler yet, getting saved, makes a person a new creature in Christ, they now have the Holy Spirit living I them. They no longer have to worry about being circumcised, or uncircumcised, anyone, anywhere, at anytime can come to Jesus for salvation if they chose to do so, that is their choice.

6:16 And as many as walk according to this rule, peace be on them, and mercy, and upon the Israel of God. For all the saved that believe this, like you and I do if you are saved, as I know I am, Paul is wishing peace and mercy on them so they can continue to spread the gospel and to live for God. It is a good and biblical thing to believe by faith on in the Lord Jesus Christ.

6:17 From henceforth let no man trouble me: for I bear in my body the marks of the Lord Jesus. Paul tells this church plainly, don't fall for the lies of the world and let this become an issue in your church anymore, I don't want to be bothered by you chasing after false gods.

Believe the word for what it says and do what the Lord ask you to do, guard your gates of your church and life and don't let in the enemy.

6:18 Brethren, the grace of our Lord Jesus Christ be with your spirit. Amen. Paul in his typical ending to a letter, he wishes them the best the Lord can give them which as you and I both know, is everything.

This has been a great study of the book of Galatians, I have learned a lot from this study, and I hope you have as well. Studying the bible is not something you will ever fully learn in your walk with the Lord, the bible is a living book, which means you may read a chapter or book in the bible now and learn a great deal from it, but in a year from now you read it again and you will see principles and truths that you did not see the first time, this is what makes the bible a living book, and that is only through the Holy Spirit living and dwelling in you.

My dear reader friend, please be intentional in your walk with God, let nothing stop you from living for the Lord his way, Satan is trying to destroy, discourage, and discredit you, stay true to the Holy Bible King James Version and you will see God do what he does. If I can ever be of assistance to you please reach out to me

You are loved

Your friend

Pastor Chris

sindestroys@gmail.com

KING JAMES BIBLE COLLEGE

My dear reader friend, I want to encourage you in your walk with the Lord. There is no greater joy than to be in the will of God. That walk must start with an absolute truth in the word of God.

God promised us in Psalms 12:6-7 that he would preserve his word to all generations, this includes you and I. With that being said I would like to invite you to consider possibly enrolling and going through the courses of King James Bible College.

All courses are only on the books of the bible condensed to forty-eight courses; no other subjects are taught but the bible. Once those courses are completed you will receive a bachelor's in bible degree from the college. This will be a valuable tool in ministry and in the service for the Lord.

This college gets a person to read their bibles, to be in their bible and to go to the bible only for all the answers. All answers are from the King James Version of the bible. All questions are true and false, multiple choice, and fill in the blanks. It is designed for the common folks to get a bible education at a very affordable price.

All courses are $30 plus a one-time registration fee of $30. These courses are available through email, website, or snail mail, you just let us know how you want them. All courses will have a video overview for the book of the bible you are studying as well as access to an instructor who can answer questions that you may have.

Please prayerfully consider enrolling in King James Bible College and let the Lord lead you how he can.

Our contact info is:
kingjamesbiblecollege@gmail.com

Thank you

You are loved

Pastor Chris Howe

President/Chairman
King James Bible College
315-466-1518

OTHER BOOKS BY THE AUTHOR

SUBJECT BOOKS:

The Office of Overseers: Biblical Church Leadership

Redemption: A True-Life Prodigal
(My personal testimony)

The genie god

The Biblical Family: From Beginning to Blended

The KJV is for Me: Why I use the King James Bible

Unguarded Gates: The Local Church

COMMENTARIES:
(Us Common Folk)

Romans

Acts

I Corinthians

II Corinthians

To Order any of these you can find them on Amazon or email me, I sell them for $10 each

Thank you
You are loved
Pastor Chris Howe

www.ingramcontent.com/pod-product-compliance
Lightning Source LLC
LaVergne TN
LVHW050553160826
845677LV00011B/2301

* 9 7 9 8 8 2 1 1 5 9 8 1 6 *